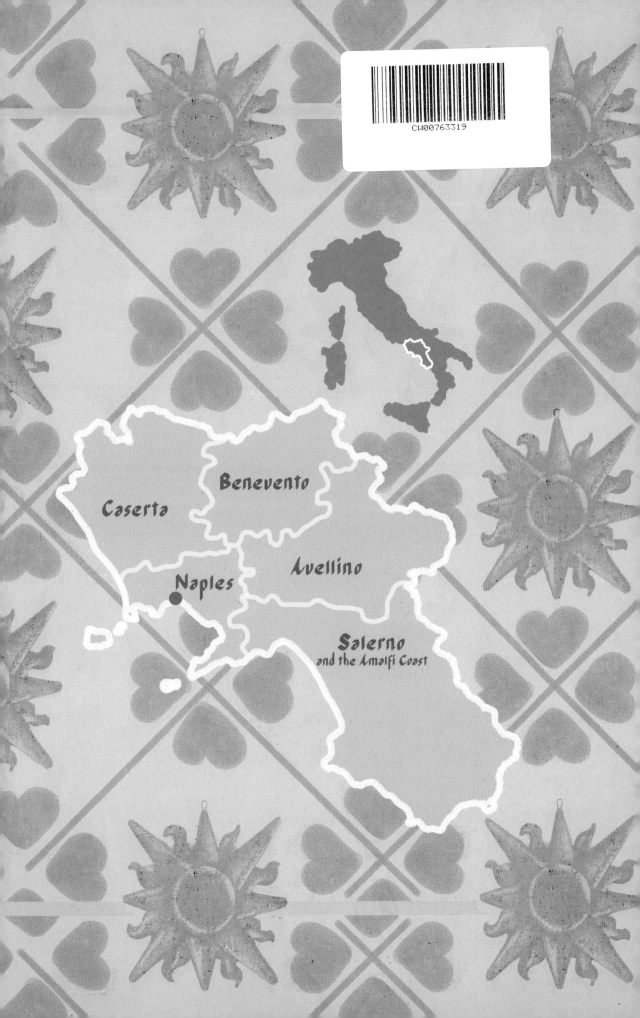

Benevento

Caserta

Avellino

Naples

Salerno
and the Amalfi Coast

The Silver Spoon

NAPLES
and the Amalfi Coast

Φ

FERTILE COUNTRYSIDE

Situated along the Gulf of Naples off the Tyrrhenian Sea in the south of Italy, there is no greater contrast than the landscape of Campania. From the hills and vineyards of Avellino and Benevento; to the temperate plains of Caserta; to the alluring and glamorous islands, cliffs, and beaches of the Amalfi Coast; to the bustling urban cultural center of Naples, Campania is an area rich in culinary pleasure. The Romans originally named Campania *campania felix*, which translates to "fertile countryside," a befitting name.

The plentiful variety of architecture, medieval towns, royal castles, and monuments showcase Campania's complex history. Because of its juxtaposition to a profitable trade route, Campania, in particular the coastal area, was settled by the Greeks in 800 BC, while the Etruscans conquered the landlocked hills and grasslands. Many wars were fought with the Samnites, primarily over possession of the Apennine mountain range. Romans organized and secured flourishing urban centers during the Roman Republic, which eventually gave way to the Byzantine Empire and rule of the Lombards, creating spectacular palaces and churches, still in existence today. Naples eventually came under Spanish rule, during which time it became the most important city in Europe, second to Paris. In 1815, after the Neapolitan War, Sicily and Naples were once again combined to create the Two Sicilies, which was considered a golden and prosperous age of culture and architecture.

The unification of Italy proved difficult for Campania's economy as a result of heavy taxation. The bombings during World War II resulted in considerable damage to Naples as well as along the coast. Campania recovered slowly and owes much of its resurgence to the tourist industry.

Page 4: The Amalfi Coast is famous for its PGI (protected geographical indication) lemons, whose enchanting aroma permeates the region.

Pages 6–7: The dramatic cliffs of the Amalfi Coast are best seen by boat.

Red peppers at a farm stand just outside of Maiori.

A tree stands tall in
a terraced garden near
Ravello.

The slumbering Mt. Vesuvius lingers in the background of nearly every view, and while majestic, it is considered the most dangerous active volcano to date, as a result of its close proximity to dense populations. The deathly eruption of 79 AD destroyed and encapsulated Pompeii and Herculaneum, both prosperous Roman centers, thus creating two major archaeological sites, noteworthy in exhibiting ancient everyday life. Not a total anathema, Mt. Vesuvius also benefits the area's soil with bountiful minerals, chalky residue, and volcanic sediment, which results in rare and celebrated varieties and crops of artichokes, zucchini, eggplant, and *friarielli* (similar to broccoli rabe). Perhaps most famously, Campania is known for two fruits: Mt. Vesuvius apricots, which grow on the slopes of the conspicuous volcano, and the fabled San Marzano, or Mt. Vesuvius, tomatoes considered the only and best tomatoes suited for true Neapolitan pizza.

The cooler air from the Apennine mountain range and fertile volcanic soil create an unparalleled terroir for vineyards, and the region of Campania boasts several consistently good wines with DOCG (controlled and guaranteed designation of origin) status, mostly heralded from Avellino, such as the bold red Taurasi and the legendary Fiano di Avellino wine, made from the ancient Fiano grape variety. Cilento, Salerno, and Sorrento all produce notable DOC (controlled designation of origin) wines.

Regional specialties result not only from the ideal marriage of climate and a unique topography, but also from the geographic location of each region. The inland territories of Avellino, Benevento, and Caserta all have hillier land and wide, expansive plains surrounded by forests. Being so removed from the sea, these regions depend on pork, particularly the rare Casertano pigs that roam Caserta, and lamb. In addition to the harvest of hazelnuts and chestnuts, utilized in a variety of sweet and savory dishes, the

Pages 12—13:
Fresh produce stands
are abundant throughout
Naples.

regions produce several fresh cheeses, such as caciocavallo and *cacioricotta*, in addition to the world-renowned DOC mozzarella di bufala, made from the treasured Caserta water buffalo.

The cuisine of the Amalfi Coast is based almost entirely on seafood as a result of the region's idyllic and vertical placement, overlooking scenic, yet working, harbors and the expansive Gulf of Naples. Dishes are often simply prepared to showcase the pure flavor of just-caught fish or shellfish. The coast is known for employing ancient fishing techniques, which lend themselves in particular to anchovy fishing and preservation, a staple flavoring agent for the cuisine of Campania. Most notably, this region is famous for its PGI (protected geographical indication) lemons, whose enchanting aroma permeates the coast: the Limone Costa d'Amalfi, which are grown on the Amalfi Coast, also called Sfusato Amalfitano, or Sorrento's Limone di Sorrento or Ovale di Sorrento. Both varieties are deeply aromatic, a bright, sunshine-hued color, and larger than any other variety of lemon. The only lemons fit for the ambrosial limoncello, a drink that epitomizes blissful summer on the Amalfi Coast.

The exuberant and energized Naples is Italy's third largest city and the capital of Campania. Not only the birthplace of the espresso machine, Naples is also the birthplace of pizza. Naples' relationship with pizza cannot be understated. This city takes its invention very seriously, with the guidance and oversight of the Associazione Verace Pizza Napoletana, an association that originated to preserve Naples' most famous culinary offering. Crunchy on the outside and soft on the inside, with a thick crust, pizzas utilizing San Marzano tomato sauces and mozzarella di bufala can be found in abundance all over Campania.

Naples is legendary for its sweet tooth, seen by the many offerings of pastries and festive holiday

Freshly baked pizza comes out of the wood-burning oven at Antica Pizzeria dal Presidente in Naples.

Page 16:
Quiet nooks appear along the narrow streets of Cusano Mutri.

Page 17:
Hilly terraced lemon gardens slope toward the ocean.

specialties, all of which require time-consuming preparations. The history of religious desserts is longstanding and paramount to Naples' culinary heritage, with fried zeppole, baked for the feast of Saint Joseph, or *pastiera napoletana*, a luscious and creamy wheat berry lattice-topped tart, served for Easter feast. Neapolitan cuisine has a tendency toward the dramatic, reflecting Naples' past history of glory and sophistication, exhibited by the historic French fusion dish of *sartù*, intricate pasta timbales, cones or wreaths of decorated Christmas *struffoli*, rum-soaked baba, and the shattering layers of *sfogliatelle*.

The vibrant history of Campania, coupled with the varied coastal and inland topography, have created a uniquely memorable region. Birthplace of several food phenomena and specialty crops, in addition to boasting copious UNESCO world sites, Campania eagerly embraces tourists. *Campania felix* is made fertile by not only Mt. Vesuvius soil, but also by a perfect trifecta of culinary accomplishment, enchanting natural beauty, and urban culture.

The streets of Vietri sul Mare are perched high up.

Pages 20–21:
The slumbering Mt. Vesuvius enriches the area's soil with minerals, chalky residue, and volcanic sediment.

FOOD FESTIVALS

Lemon granita can be found at roadside stands throughout the Amalfi Coast.

There is no better way to embark on a culinary journey through Campania than by attending or visiting a *sagra*, or festival. *Sagre* (which comes from the Latin for holy) were originally religious community events that took place in churches; and though many *sagre* still occur in accordance with the Catholic church calendar, most are now food festivals, highly important to the tourism industry. There are of course *sagre* that celebrate both religious and edible events, like the feast day of Saint Joseph, where Campania's famous zeppole are served to appreciative crowds.

Some *sagre* celebrate a prized ingredient common to all Campania, such as the eggplant (aubergine) or Naples' famous invention of pizza. But many *sagre* are highly specific, such as a festival honoring fusilli pasta or bluefish. The festivals also exhibit the Italians' deep sense of community and desire to come together over food or a meal. Often occurring in town squares or centers, these festivals are meant to be enjoyed by natives and visitors alike.

Campania festivals extol the various DOC wines or grape harvests, lemons, olive oil, and fresh cheeses such as caciocavalli, mozzarella di bufala, and fior di latte, all of which play an essential role in Campania's local diet. Special attention is also paid to the coastline's wealth of just-caught seafood and the inner region's appreciation of pork. The perfect partnership of climate and mineral-rich volcanic soil from Mt. Vesuvius create a fertile environment for many unique regional crops (such as apricots, cherries, artichokes, tomatoes, and chestnuts), most of which have a short season. Thus *sagre* are also an opportunity to urge attendees to celebrate an ingredient before it disappears until next year.

Pages 26–27: Fields of sunflowers grow in Benevento.

A list of food festivals within Campania is on the following pages.

FOOD FESTIVALS

JANUARY

O cippo di Sant'Antonio | Festival of Saint Anthony
Naples, Naples

La ruzzola del formaggio | Cheese Throwing Festival
Pontelandolfo, Benevento

MARCH

Festa di San Giuseppe | Feast Day of St. Joseph
Throughout Campania

Disfida del soffritto di maiale | Pork Soup Cook-Off
Irpino, Avellino

APRIL

Festa carciofi | Artichoke Festival
Paestum, Salerno

MAY

Wine and the city | Wine and the City
Naples, Naples

Le strade della mozzarella | The Many Roads
of Mozzarella
Paestum, Salerno

JUNE

Vinischia | Vinischia
Ischia, Naples

Festa della pizza | Pizza Festival
Montoro Superiore, Avellino

Sagra dell'albicocca | Apricot Festival
Sant'anastasia, Naples

Sagra del pesce fritto | Fried Fish Festival
Castellammare Di Stabia, Naples

Sagra della ciliegia | Cherry Festival
Forchia, Benevento

Sagra del fusillo | Fusilli Festival
Nocera Inferiore, Salerno

Sagra degli gnocchi | Gnocchi Festival
Pantuliano, Caserta

JULY

Sagra del tonno | Tuna Festival
Cetara, Salerno

Sagra del limone | Lemon Festival
Massa Lubrense, Naples

Sagra dei fusilli e del pecorino | Fusilli and Pecorino
Festival
Ceppaloni, Benevento

Sagra del pomodorino | Tomato Festival
Corbara, Salerno

Sagra del peperone ripieno | Stuffed Peppers Festival
San Martino Sannita, Benevento

AUGUST

Sagra del prosciutto e dei fichi | Prosciutto
and Figs Festival
Castel San Giorgio, Salerno

Festa del grano | Wheat Harvest Festival
Foglianise, Benevento

Sagra del pesce azzurro | Blue Fish Festival
Atrani and Sapri, Salerno

Sagra delle melanzane al cassone | Eggplant Festival
Montesarchio, Benevento

Sagra dei cicatielli e del pane di montecalvo |
Cicatielli and Montecalvo Bread Festival
Irpinia, Avellino

Sagra della mozzarella ind'à murtedda |
Mozzarella Festival
Velia, Salerno

Fiordilatte fiordifesta | Feast of Fior di Latte
Agerola, Salerno

Sagra della sfogliatella di Santa Rosa |
Sfogliatella of Santa Rosa Festival
Conca dei Marini, Salerno

Sagra del fusillo e della braciola | Fusilli and
Braciole Festival
Pietradefusi, Avellino

Sagra del mare Flegrea | Festival of the Sea
Procida, Naples

Festa della melanzana alla cioccolata |
Chocolate Eggplant Festival
Maiori, Salerno

SEPTEMBER

Sagra del fungo porcino | Porcini Festival
Montoro Superiore, Avellino

Gusta Minori | A Taste of Minori
Minori, Salerno

Settembrata Anacaprese | Grape Harvest
Festival of Anacapri
Capri, Naples

Sagra dell'uva | Grape Festival
Capri, Naples

Pizzafest | Pizzafest
Fuorigrotta, Naples

Napoli pizza village | Napoli Pizza Village
Naples, Naples

Sagra del fico d'india | Prickly Pear Festival
Castel Morrone, Caserta

Sagra del caciocavallo | Caciocavallo Festival
Castelfranco in Miscano, Benevento

Festa della vendemmia | Grape Harvest Festival
Tramonti, Salerno

Festa del pesce | Feast of the Fish
Positano, Salerno

OCTOBER

Festa della castagne | Feast of the Chestnuts
Scala, Salerno

Sagra dell'olio d'oliva | Olive Oil Festival
Cervino, Caserta

Sagra del tartufo e della castagna | Black Truffles
and Chestnuts Festival
Irpinia, Avellino

NOVEMBER

Festa di Sant'Antonio | Feast of St. Andrew
Amalfi, Salerno

Il mosto che diventa vino | The Must that
Becomes Wine
Tramonti, Salerno

DECEMBER

Sagra della salsiccia e ceppone | Sausage and
Bonfire Festival
Sorrento, Naples

Festa del Torrone | Feast of the Torrone
San Marco dei Cavoti, Benevento

Sagra della scarpegghia | Scarpegghia Festival
Calitri, Avellino

Sagra della zeppola | Zeppole Festival
Positano, Salerno

NAPLES

NAPLES

The area around the Gulf of Naples is the most populous region of Campania, and includes the vibrant and intense urban center of Naples, which rises from the bay up to the precipitous, surrounding hills. Italy's third largest city and the capital of Campania, Naples is a city of many contrasts: Its labyrinth of ancient Roman streets creates a difficult traffic experience, making it unpleasant and chaotic to navigate; yet the city has many acclaimed institutions and is rich with celebrated architecture. Until the unification of Italy in the nineteenth century, Naples was the pinnacle of Italian cultural life; but then the city's wealth was repurposed to fund the northern industrial expansion, and Naples' power was weakened.

Naples today is a vibrant and welcoming city best explored on foot. Wander the Spanish Quarter to experience the older version of Naples, complete with a view into what life once was. Explore such cultural highlights as Piazza del Plebiscito, the most beautiful and majestic piazza and neoclassical church in Naples, which serves as the heart of Naples, or the imposing waterside castle, Castel Nuovo, also known as Maschio Angioini.

With a long Roman and Greek history dating from the second millennium BC, Naples is rich with legend. Castle dell'Ovo, or "Castle of the Egg," built on an island in the ninth century BC, alludes to the tale of Virgil placing an egg under the castle to protect it. This longstanding fortress (a royal residence until the twentieth century) is a waterfront symbol of the city.

The region around Naples boasts many fertile lands and vineyards, mostly as a result of the mineral-rich and chalky volcanic soil. Mt. Vesuvius remains an actively dangerous, yet slumbering volcano to the east of Naples. Both the city of Pompeii and the resort town of Herculaneum are a vestige of what Roman

A colorful array of seafood at a fish market.

life was like before being covered by Vesuvius'
eruption of deadly ash, toxic gas, and molten lava in
79 AD. Both areas were buried and fossilized, and thus
preserved. Both Ischia (a volcanic island famous for
its thermal baths) and the Phlegraen Fields (a regional
park with hydrothermal activity, ruins, and ancient
fishing towns) can also be visited. Mt. Vesuvius has
also created an excellent landscape for vineyards (with
many high-quality DOC wines) and the perfect
growing conditions for superior San Marzano tomatoes
and the impossibly sweet Mt. Vesuvius apricots.

The Naples region also boasts the glamorous,
aristocratic retreat of Capri, a tiny island with myriad
caves, grand villas, and sunbaked terraced gardens. The
magically beautiful Blue Grotto, an azure-colored sea
cave (and a temple in Roman times) is a popular
tourist attraction. Capri's dramatic limestone cliffs
flank an intoxicatingly clear, turquoise sea.

Right across from Capri, at the southern end of the
Gulf of Naples, lies Sorrento, another prominent
coastal tourist destination often considered the
gateway to the Amalfi Coast. Sorrento boasts unob-
structed views of Capri, Naples, and Mt. Vesuvius.
Awash in enchanting yellow lemon trees with gardens
precariously balanced on cliffs, legend has it that
Sorrento is the rocky site where sirens wrecked
travelers in Homer's *The Odyssey*. Famous for its PGI
(protected geographical indication) lemons—Limone
di Sorrento or Ovale di Sorrento—Sorrento is
engulfed in a citrus aroma.

In the region of Naples, local cuisine reigns supreme.
Known as the birthplace of pizza, ragu, Mt. Vesuvius
tomatoes, and limoncello, Naples' dedication and
contributions to the culinary arts is matchless. Naples
is the home to the original espresso machine as well
as memorable pastries and cakes such as baba, *pastiera*,
sfogliatella, and *struffoli*.

Pages 34—35:
The eighteenth-century
obelisk of San Domenico,
or Saint Dominic, stands
tall in the center of Piazza
San Domenico Maggiore.

SALSA GENOVESE

Not to be confused with pesto Genovese, this iconic Neapolitan pasta sauce requires long, slow cooking. It is most often served with ziti, a tubular pasta that captures this rich sauce in its hollow center, though it can also be served with similar-shaped pastas such as penne.

Preparation time: 20 minutes
Cooking time: 2 hours 30 minutes
Serves 6

Heat the oil, lard, and prosciutto in a saucepan. Add the onions, celery, and carrot and cook, stirring for 10 minutes. Add the beef, cover, and cook over low heat for at least 1 hour. Increase the heat and sauté the meat. Season with salt and pepper. Add half the wine and cook until it evaporates. Add the remaining wine and cook until it evaporates again.

Stir the tomato paste with a few spoonfuls of hot water to loosen it up. Add the tomato paste to the pan juices and cook for 1 hour, drizzling in a little hot water as necessary, until the vegetables are shiny and dark and the sauce is reduced. Remove the meat from the pot and set aside for the main course. Toss the onion sauce with pasta and serve as a first course.

Genovese sauce

— 5 tablespoons (75 ml) olive oil
— 5 tablespoons (70 g) lard or butter
— 3½ oz (100 g) prosciutto, finely diced
— 5½ lb (2 kg) onions, thinly sliced
— 1 stalk celery, diced
— 1 carrot, diced
— 2¼ lb (1 kg) bottom round (silverside), trussed with kitchen string
— salt and pepper
— ¾ cup (200 ml) red wine
— 1 teaspoon tomato paste (purée)

GONFIETTI

Fried dough with anchovies

— 1 envelope (¼ oz/7 g)
   active dry yeast
— ¼ cup (75 ml) warm water
— pinch of granulated sugar
— 2 cups (250 g) all-purpose
   (plain) flour
— 1 tablespoon olive oil
— 3½ oz (100 g) anchovy fillets
— about ¼ cup peanut or
   canola oil, for shallow-frying

Preparation time: 20 minutes + 1 hour 15 minutes rising
Cooking time: 30 minutes
Makes 16–20

Dissolve the yeast in a bowl with the water and sugar. Set aside for 15 minutes.

Stir in the flour and olive oil and knead until the dough is smooth and elastic, about 2 minutes. Cover and let rise in a warm place for 1 hour.

Remove any bones from the anchovy fillets and chop them. Knead the anchovies into the dough. On a floured surface, roll the dough out into a thin sheet about ¼ inch (6 mm) thick. Use a 2½-inch (6 cm) round cutter to cut into rounds. Re-roll any scraps and cut out more rounds.

Heat the oil in a 12-inch (30 cm) frying pan over medium-high heat until hot. Working in batches, shallow-fry half the dough rounds until golden brown, 1–1½ minutes per side. Repeat with the remaining rounds, adding more oil if necessary. Remove the *gonfietti* and drain them thoroughly on a plate lined with paper towels. Serve hot.

PIZZELLE FRITTE

Preparation time: 15 minutes + 2 hours rising
Cooking time: 30 minutes
Makes 16

To make the dough: Combine the yeast, water, and salt in a large bowl and stir to dissolve. Add the flour and olive oil and stir until combined. Kneading the dough for 1–2 minutes, form into a ball, cover the bowl with a cloth, and set aside in a warm place to rise, kneading the dough after 1 hour, and setting it aside for another hour until the dough has doubled in volume.

Divide the dough into 16 portions. Form into balls and pat them into small oval shapes, about 3 inches (7.5 cm) long and 1 inch (2.5 cm) thick.

Heat the ¼ cup (60 ml) oil in a large 12-inch (30 cm) frying pan. Working in batches, fry the *pizzelle* until browned on all sides, 2–3 minutes. Repeat with the remaining *pizzelle*, adding more oil if necessary. Remove with a slotted spoon and drain on paper towels.

To serve, arrange the *pizzelle* in layers on a serving dish and top each with 1 tablespoon tomato sauce and about 1 teaspoon Parmesan. Serve hot.

Fried pizzelle

For the dough:
— 1 envelope (¼ oz/7 g) active dry yeast
— 1¼ cups (295 ml) warm water
— pinch of salt
— 4 cups plus 2 tablespoons (500 g) all-purpose (plain) flour
— 1 tablespoon olive oil

For cooking and serving:
— about ¼ cup (60 ml) olive oil, for frying
— 1 cup (235 ml) tomato sauce (from Ravioli Capresi, page 60)
— grated Parmesan cheese

TIMPANO DI RIGATONI IN PIEDI

Rigatoni mold

For the meat sauce
— 3½ tablespoons (50 ml) olive oil
— 1 small yellow onion, thinly sliced
— 1 lb 2 oz (500 g) ground beef (90–93% lean)
— 3½ cups (830 ml) tomato sauce (from Ravioli Capresi, page 60)
— salt and pepper

For the dough
— 3½ cups (450 g) all-purpose (plain) flour
— 13 tablespoons (6½ oz/ 180 g) butter, at room temperature
— ¾ cup (175 ml) warm water
— pinch of salt

For the rigatoni and filling
— 10 oz (300 g) rigatoni
— generous ¾ cup (7 oz/200 g) ricotta cheese
— 9 oz (250 g) fior di latte or fresh mozzarella cheese, cubed →

Preparation time: 45 minutes + 30 minutes rising
Cooking time: 3 hours 50 minutes
Serves 8–10

To make the meat sauce: Heat the oil in a medium saucepan. Add the onion and cook until tender, about 3 minutes. Add the ground meat and cook, breaking it up with a spoon, until no longer pink, 3–5 minutes. Add the tomato sauce and bring to a boil. Reduce to a simmer and cook over very low heat for 3 hours, stirring occasionally and seasoning with salt and pepper to taste.

In the meantime, to make the dough: Pile the flour on a work surface and create a well in the center. Add the butter, water, and salt. Knead together all the ingredients, adding more water if needed, until a smooth and even dough is obtained, about 5 minutes. Cover and let rest for 30 minutes.

To prepare the rigatoni: Cook the rigatoni in a large pot of boiling water until al dente and drain.

Meanwhile, for the rigatoni filling, stir together the ricotta, fior di latte, and ½ cup (120 ml) of meat sauce.

Cut off one-quarter of the dough and set aside. Roll out the larger piece of dough into a rectangle, then roll it up and then coil it up (like a snail). Flatten and roll out again to a round that will fit a mold 8 inches round by 4 inches deep (22 cm x 10 cm) or standard springform pan.

Preheat the oven to 400°F (200°C/Gas Mark 6). Lightly grease the mold or springform pan.

For the timpano

— 3 ½ oz (100 g) cooked ham,
   thinly sliced
— 5 oz (150 g) fior di latte
   mozzarella cheese,
   thinly sliced
— 2 tablespoons grated
   Parmesan cheese

To assemble the *timpano*: Stuff each rigatoni with the cheese filling and stand half of them up vertically, one close to the other, proceeding in concentric circles from the outside inwards, in the dough-lined mold. Arrange half of the ham in the mold. Top with half the fior di latte and Parmesan. Repeat with the remaining filled rigatoni and top with the remaining ham, fior di latte, and Parmesan. Top with the meat sauce and smooth into an even layer.

To make the "lid" for the *timpano*, roll the reserved piece of dough into a round that will fit the top of the mold. Place it over the filling, tucking in the edges and sealing it well. Bake for 40 minutes. Turn off the oven and leave the *timpano* in for 10 minutes. Remove from the oven and release it from the mold to serve.

RAGU

Page 45:
Neapolitans fishing along a section of the city's vast waterfront marinas.

Ragu is a deeply savory meat-based tomato sauce, often served with pasta. This satiating sauce requires hours of simmering, releasing an intensely pleasing aroma as it cooks, and most families from Campania hold their own family recipe close. Large cuts of meat, such as pork or beef ribs or shoulder, can be added to the tomato sauce, and then later removed once tender and served alongside the ragu-tossed pasta. Occasionally regional sausages are included. The most common version of today's ragu is made with ground beef or pork. However, two versions exist: *ragù alla napoletana* and *ragù bolognese*. *Ragù alla napoletana* is made with sautéed onions, garlic, whole cuts of meat, and tomato sauce, whereas *ragù bolognese* uses minced or ground meat and less onion. The Neapolitan version includes red wine, olive oil, and basil whereas Bolognese excludes any herbs. Bolognese is a much more minimal sauce, whereas Neapolitan is more flexible, often using different flavorings such as pine nuts and raisins, or milk or cream to enrich the sauce.

It is believed that ragu is derived from the French *ragoûts* of Emilia-Romagna during the late eighteenth century. The first *ragù* recipe was recorded by Alberto Alvisi at that time. Ragu also appeared in cookbooks from Emilia-Romagna in the mid-1800s. By the late nineteenth century, serving and cooking ragu was tradition for holidays and important occasions, as well as on Sundays for wealthier families. Eventually, pasta became more popular and affordable after World War II. The American version of ragu, or "Sunday gravy," most likely originated from the Neapolitan favorite, with more meat.

Ragu is a traditional Sunday meal for many Neapolitans, infusing the city's streets with its aroma. The sauce is used to dress pasta, while the meat is eaten as a main course.

Rice timbale with meat sauce

Preparation time: 2 hours
Cooking time: 2 hours
Serves 12

For the meat sauce
— 4 tablespoons olive oil
— 1 yellow onion, chopped
— 2 stalks celery, chopped
— 2 carrots, chopped
— 3½ oz (100 g)
    prosciutto, minced
— 1 lb 5 oz (600 g) ground
    (minced) veal
— ½ cup (120 ml), dry
    white wine
— 2 tablespoons tomato
    paste (purée)
— ¾–1 cup (175–240 ml)
    beef stock
— salt and pepper

For the meatballs
— 1 slice bread
— 3½ oz (100 g) ground
    (minced) veal
— 1 egg yolk
— ½ teaspoon chopped parsley
— pinch of salt
— ½ cup (120 ml) olive oil →

To make the meat sauce: Heat the oil in a medium frying pan over medium-high heat. Add the chopped vegetables and prosciutto, reduce the heat to low, and cook for 2−3 minutes. Add the veal, increase the heat to medium-high, and cook, breaking up the meat, about 3 minutes. Add the wine and deglaze the pan. Cook until the wine has evaporated. Dilute the tomato paste with a little water and add to the pan. Add enough stock to cover the mixture and season with salt and pepper. Cover and simmer for about 1 hour, stirring occasionally, and adding more stock if the sauce begins to look too dry. The sauce must be thick at the end of cooking. Taste for seasoning.

To make the meatballs: Wet the bread with the water, squeeze out the liquid, and add to a bowl. Add the veal, egg yolk, parsley, and salt and mix thoroughly to combine. Taking a little mixture at a time, form small meatballs about the size of a hazelnut.

Heat a large frying pan over medium-high heat and add the oil. Once warm, fry the meatballs 2 minutes on the first side. Flip and cook until golden brown and cooked through, about 1 more minute. Remove the meatballs from the oil with a slotted spoon and drain on a plate lined with paper towels.

To make the risotto: Melt 2 tablespoons of the butter in a medium-large saucepan over medium-high heat. Add the rice and stir to coat in the butter. Pour in the stock and wine, season to taste with salt and pepper, and bring to a boil. Reduce to a simmer and cook for 10−12 minutes. The risotto will be partially cooked at this point. Remove the pan from the heat and stir in the remaining 2 tablespoons butter, the Parmesan,

For the risotto

— 4 tablespoons
   (2 oz/55 g) butter
— 3¾ cups (26 oz/750 g)
   Arborio or carnaroli rice
— 3¾ cups (890 ml)
   chicken stock
— ½cup (120 ml) dry
   white wine
— salt and pepper
— scant 1 cup (80 g) grated
   Parmesan cheese
— 3 eggs

For the timbale

— ¼cup (20 g) dried mushrooms
— 4 tablespoons
   (2 oz/55 g) butter
— 2 oz (50 g) cooked ham,
   minced
— 2 hard-boiled eggs, chopped
— 5 oz (150 g) mozzarella
   cheese, cut into cubes
— 1½ cups (200 g) peas
— 5 oz (150 g) sweet Italian
   pork sausage, cooked
   and crumbled
— pepper
— scant 1 cup (80 g)
   grated Parmesan cheese
— ¼–½ cup (30–60 g)
   breadcrumbs

eggs, and pepper to taste. If desired, stir in a few spoonfuls of the meat sauce. Taste for seasoning.

Measure out enough of the risotto to cover the top of the timbale and set aside. Spread the rest of the risotto over the bottom and up the sides of a 9-inch (23 cm) springform pan, pressing down with a spoon so that it adheres well, to make a shell.

Preheat the oven to 400°F (200°C/Gas Mark 6). Line a baking sheet with foil.

To prepare the timbale: In a small bowl, pour hot water over the dried mushrooms and let reconstitute, about 5 minutes. Drain and chop.

Heat a small frying pan over medium-high heat. Add 2 tablespoons of the butter and once melted, add the mushrooms and ham. Sauté until heated through, about 5 minutes.

To assemble the timbale, fill the middle of the risotto shell with the hard-boiled eggs, mozzarella, peas, mushroom and ham mixture, crumbled sausage, and meatballs. Season with pepper.

Measure out one-third of the meat sauce and set aside for serving later. Alternately layer in the Parmesan and remaining meat sauce. Cover with the reserved risotto, smoothing the top with a spatula. Sprinkle the breadcrumbs on top in an even layer and dot with cubes of the remaining 2 tablespoons butter.

Place the pan on the lined baking sheet. Cover the top of the timbale with more foil and bake for about 1 hour. About 15 minutes before the timbale is ready, remove the foil to slightly brown the top. Take the timbale out of the oven and, after 15 minutes, carefully release the sides of the pan and transfer to a hot serving dish. Thin the reserved meat sauce with a little stock and serve it in a sauceboat alongside the timbale.

RICE

Page 51:
A shop sells regional products like dried pastas, buffalo mozzarella, and provolone del Monaco.

While pasta is typically preferred in southern Italy, rice or *riso* is featured in a variety of regional dishes. Traditionally paired with plentiful Campania seafood, rice is featured in *sartù di riso al ragù* (Rice Timbale with Meat Sauce, page 48), in which a rice shell encases a textured and decadent filling of eggs, ham, meatballs, peas, mushrooms, and mozzarella; swathed in a traditional ragu.

The *sartù* is an imitation of a French dish, and comes from the word *surtout*, which translates to "above all." Often described as one of the first French and Italian fusion dishes in Naples, the timbale comes in two versions: *rosso*, a red and more popular version, and *bianco*, a white version with no sauce.

Rice provides a nutty flavor and mild heft to salads, which often feature fresh seafood with punchy flavor additions such as currants, pine nuts, and fresh herbs. *Suppli di riso*, rice balls, are a favorite street food, available at shops and stands throughout the city of Naples. Like a rice timbale, these plump and deeply savory balls feature a variety of fillings. Dipped in breadcrumbs and then fried, *suppli di riso* are an irresistible treat.

Several varieties of rice can be used depending on the dish being prepared. Medium-grain rice is used in popular Italian risotto dishes, specifically Arborio rice. Long-grain rice is better suited for dishes that require the rice to keep its shape and bite; whereas short-grain rice melts into creamy dessert dishes.

Rice is the star of one of Neapolitan cooking's most emblematic dishes, the rice timbale, or *sartù di riso.*

Seafood timbale

For the pasta
— 1 lb (450 g) spaghetti
— 7 tablespoons (100 ml)
   olive oil
— 1 clove garlic, peeled
   but whole
— 2 tablespoons breadcrumbs
— Chopped parsley, to taste
— 3½ oz (100 g) anchovy fillets,
   chopped

For the filling
— 9 tablespoons (130 ml)
   olive oil
— 2 cloves garlic, peeled
   but whole
— 5 oz (150 g) mushrooms,
   thinly sliced
— 2¼ lb (1 kg) mussels
— 1 can (28 oz/795 g) San
   Marzano tomatoes, drained,
   juiced, seeded, and chopped
— ½ cup (120 ml) dry white wine
— 5 tablespoons capers, rinsed
— 3½ oz (100 g) pitted black
   olives, halved
— 1 lb (454 g) peas
— 11 oz (300 g) shrimp
   (prawns), peeled and
   deveined
— 7 oz (200 g) baby squid,
   sliced into 1-inch
   (2.5 cm) rounds
— ¼ cup chopped parsley
— salt and pepper →

A timbale in Naples is known as a *timpano*.
Throughout the rest of Italy a timbale is known as a
timballo. Timpano is also the name for the mold (once
made from tin-plated iron and now from steel) used
to make the dish. The name comes from timpanum,
a percussion instrument with a hemispherical shape
similar to a timbale. This timbale is meatless, hence
the word *scammaro*, which refers to the religious days
of abstaining from meat.

Preparation time: 1 hour 15 minutes
Cooking time: 45 minutes
Serves 6−8

To prepare the pasta: Cook the pasta in a large pot
of unsalted water until al dente. Drain and set aside.

Heat the olive oil in a large frying pan. Add the garlic
clove and brown. Add the breadcrumbs and when
they are golden brown, about 3 minutes, add parsley
to taste and the anchovies. Immediately remove from
the heat and stir to break up the anchovies. Discard
the whole garlic clove. Transfer the cooked pasta to
the pan with the breadcrumb mixture toss until
combined. Return to the stove and cook for a few
minutes over very low heat.

Preheat the oven to 350°F (180°C/Gas Mark 4).
Line a baking sheet with foil.

To make the filling: Heat 2 tablespoons of the oil in
a large frying pan over medium-high heat. Add one
of the garlic cloves and brown. Add the mushrooms
and sauté until golden brown and tender, about
5 minutes. Remove the mushrooms from the pan
and set aside. Discard the whole garlic clove.

— Olive oil, for brushing

— ¼–½ cup (30–60 g)
  breadcrumbs

— 1½ tablespoons (20 g)
  butter or lard, cubed

Meanwhile, scrub and rinse the mussels. Debeard the mussels, if needed, and discard any mussels that will not close.

In the same pan used to cook the mushrooms, heat 3½ tablespoons of the oil and brown the remaining garlic clove. Add the mussels, cover, and cook, shaking the pan occasionally, until they open, 5–6 minutes. Remove from the heat and discard any mussels that have not opened. Then remove the meats from the shells. Strain the cooking liquid into a bowl.

In the same pan that was used for the mushrooms, heat the remaining 3 ½ tablespoons oil over medium heat. Add the drained and chopped tomatoes, strained mussel cooking liquid, and the wine. Cook until the liquid has almost evaporated, about 5 to 7 minutes. Return the mushrooms to the pan, along with the capers, olives, and peas. Cook for 2–3 minutes. Add the shrimp (prawns), squid, parsley, and salt and pepper to taste. Cook until the seafood is just cooked through, 2–3 minutes. The sauce should be thick. Remove from the heat and add the mussel meats.

To prepare the mold: Generously brush a 9-inch (23 cm) springform pan with olive oil. Evenly coat with 3 tablespoons of the breadcrumbs.

Arrange three-quarters of the pasta in the prepared pan, leaving a large hole in the center. Using a slotted spoon, scoop the seafood mixture into the center, leaving any remaining liquid behind in the pot. Cover with the remaining pasta, level off the surface and sprinkle with plenty of breadcrumbs. Dot the top evenly with the butter. Cover with foil and bake on the lined baking sheet for 30 minutes. Remove the foil and bake until the breadcrumbs are browned, about 15 minutes longer. Remove from the oven and let the timbale stand for about 15 minutes. Use a knife to loosen the timbale and carefully remove the sides of the springform pan. Serve hot.

PASTA

Northern Italy mostly favors fresh, homemade pasta made with eggs, and Southern Italy is known for its variety of dried pastas, known as *maccheroni*, made from hard durum wheat. Whereas pasta was not created in Campania, and the region is only the sixth largest producer today, some of the world's best pasta shapes and varieties were created in Campania.

Semolina, milled from durum wheat, is used to make pasta. The mild breezes from the Gulf of Naples and hot winds from Mt. Vesuvius not only encourage durum wheat crops, but also ensure that the pasta dries well and does not mold or break. It was a common sight in Naples throughout the eighteenth century to see pasta being hung throughout the city on poles or sold by street vendors.

Industrial production began in the area of Gragnano, inland of the Amalfi Coast, which developed drying and preservation techniques and shaped the pasta into spaghetti, linguine, ziti, and *paccheri*, specialty pasta shaped like a large tube. Pasta was produced commercially in the fifteenth century and is still produced today according to traditional methods, although only a few producers remain true to ancient production methods. In a method called *trafilata a bronzo*, pasta dough is forced through bronze dies to create a variety of shapes. This helps create a porous surface, providing ample opportunities for the pasta to catch sauce.

Historically, the upper class consumed pastas on holidays or used the ingredient in elaborate dishes, such as timbales. Less wealthy classes would mix smaller amounts of pasta with beans, as meat was too expensive. Popular San Marzano tomatoes provide excellent sauces, such as *ragù* or *sugo*, which are often paired with pasta. Seafood is a primary accompaniment to pasta throughout the region, considering the proximity to the sea.

Page 57: A colorful street market sells seasonal produce.

The hillside town of Gragnano is considered to be the birthplace of dried pasta.

RAVIOLI CAPRESI

Capresi ravioli

For the tomato sauce
— 3 tablespoons olive oil
— 2 cloves garlic, peeled but whole
— 1 can (28 oz/795 g) San Marzano tomatoes, drained and halved
— pinch of salt

For the filling
— 3½ oz (100 g) aged provolone cheese, grated (1 ½ cups)
— 1 egg yolk
— 3–4 marjoram or sage leaves, shredded
— 2 teaspoons grated Parmesan cheese
— salt and pepper
— basil leaves, chopped

For the pasta
— 4¾ cups (500 g) 00 flour
— pinch of salt
— 1 egg yolk
— 3 tablespoons olive oil
— hot water, as needed

— grated Parmesan cheese, for serving

Preparation time: 1 hour
Cooking time: 20 minutes
Serves 6

To make the sauce: Heat the oil in a medium saucepan over medium-high heat, add the garlic cloves and brown, about 2 minutes. Remove and discard the garlic. Add the tomatoes and salt and cook for 10 minutes, then mash them with a fork and cook the sauce over high heat until thick, 7–10 minutes.

While the sauce is cooking, make the filling: Mash the provolone with a fork and stir in the egg yolk, shredded marjoram, and Parmesan. Season with salt and pepper to taste and sprinkle in some basil.

To make the pasta: Pile the flour on a work surface and create a well in the center. Add the salt and egg yolk. Blend in a little flour at a time, pour in the oil and knead the mixture, gradually adding 1 tablespoon of hot water at a time until the dough forms a ball. Knead until the dough is smooth and elastic, 2–4 minutes. Divide the dough in half and, on a floured surface, roll out 2 rounds 18 inches (45 cm) across and about ⅛ inch (4 mm) thick.

Place 1 teaspoon-size mounds of filling in evenly spaced rows onto one round of dough. Cover with the other sheet of dough, press with the fingers around the filling to seal and release the air. Cut out ravioli with a 1–1 ½-inch (2.5–4 cm) round pastry cutter.

Bring a large pot of salted water to a boil. Add the ravioli in batches, pressing any loose seams together before cooking. Boil until the ravioli turn opaque and float to the top, 4–6 minutes. With a slotted spoon, transfer to the pan with the sauce.

Serve with Parmesan sprinkled on top.

BACCALÀ ALLA
PERPICAREGNA

Preparation time: 20 minutes + 24 hours soaking
Cooking time: 30 minutes
Serves 4

Soak the salt cod in a bowl of water in the refrigerator for 24 hours, periodically changing the water. Drain well.

Put at least one 1 inch of water in the bottom of a steamer. Cover and bring to boil. Lay the cod on the steamer's rack, cover again, and cook for about 10 minutes. Remove from the pan, allow the fish to cool a little, then flake and remove the bones.

Heat the oil in a frying pan with the garlic. Add the peppers and cook until crunchy. Remove and cut out the stem and the seeds. (Discard the garlic and oil.)

Arrange the flakes of cod and the peppers on a platter and serve.

Perpicaregna-style salt cod

— 1 lb (450 g) salt cod
— 7 tablespoons (100 ml) olive oil
— 1–2 cloves garlic, peeled but whole
— 8 dried sweet green peppers

SALT COD

An important dish to Southern Italians is *baccalà*, or salt cod. Traditionally eaten on Fridays by Catholics, or considered a Christmas Eve tradition, salt cod can be prepared in a variety of ways.

Before preserving cod in salt, the fresh fish is filleted. Cod preserved by drying is called *stoccafisso* and cod that is salt-cured is *baccalà*. If possible, purchase presoaked *baccalà*, which yields a meatier and firmer textured fish with a pure aroma. If *baccalà* is bought dry, it must be soaked and rehydrated in fresh, cold water, and refrigerated for twenty-four to forty-eight hours, changing the water and rinsing the fish every few hours. In Italy, most markets and fishmongers have large marble sinks in which *baccalà* is piled under trickling, cold water; a memorable sight for market tourists and shoppers.

Baccalà is ready for cooking once it is white in color and puffy in texture. Preparation is often simple and light. The fish is usually served with tomatoes, peppers, potatoes, and eggplant (aubergine), and is the perfect accompaniment to spicy tomato sauce. *Baccalà alla napoletana* is fried salt cod, served with a simple tomato sauce flavored with traditional Neapolitan ingredients such as olives, capers, and nuts. The fish can also be tossed with lemon, garlic, and parsley, or tucked into *pizza di baccalà* (Salt Cod Pizza, page 196) as a light filling combined with capers and anchovies.

Page 62:
Naples's oldest castle, Castel dell'Ovo, or Castle of the Egg, was built by the Normans in the twelfth century.

Page 63:
The Bay of Naples extends twenty miles (32 km) from Cape Miseno to Campanella Point.

Once preserved in salt, cod becomes a pantry staple that will last for a very long time without spoiling.

CONIGLIO ALL'ISCHITANA

Ischitana-style rabbit

— 3 lb 6 oz (1.5 kg) rabbit
  pieces, liver and other offal
  kept separate
— 1 cup (250 ml) dry white wine
— about ½ cup (120 ml) olive oil
— 4 cloves garlic, unpeeled
— handful of very large basil
  leaves
— 2 tablespoons lard
— 15 cherry tomatoes, quartered
— salt and pepper
— fresh herbs, for garnish

Preparation time: 20 minutes + 2 hours marinating
Cooking time: 1 hour
Serves 6

Add the rabbit pieces to a bowl, cover with the wine and set aside to marinate for about 2 hours. Drain and reserve the marinade.

Heat the oil in a deep sauté pan, add the garlic and brown. Remove and discard the garlic. Add the rabbit and brown each piece on all sides. Drizzle with ⅔ cup (150 ml) of the marinade and cook until it evaporates. Wrap the pieces of liver and offal in the basil leaves to form small rolls and place in the pan with the rabbit pieces. Add the lard and tomatoes to the pan, season with salt and pepper, and cook over medium heat for about 40 minutes, adding hot water if the pan gets too dry. Adjust the seasoning.

Serve on a platter. Garnish with aromatic herbs, such as basil, sage, rosemary, or wild fennel.

POLPO ALLA LUCIANA

Preparation time: 20 minutes
Cooking time: 2 hours
Serves 4

Place the octopus in a Dutch oven (casserole) and
add the olive oil, lemon slices, parsley, and chili pepper
and season with salt and black pepper. Cover the dish
with a sheet of parchment paper, securing it firmly
with kitchen string, place the lid on top, and cook over
medium heat for about 2 hours (without removing the
lid). Remove from the heat, let the octopus cool
in the dish, then cut into pieces and rounds and serve
with its sauce (it is also good warm or even cold).

*Luciana-style
octopus*

— 1½–2 lb (450–680 g)
  octopus, cleaned
— generous ¾ cup (200 ml) olive
  oil
— 1 lemon, sliced
— 1 sprig parsley, chopped
— 1 fresh red chili pepper,
  sliced into thin rings
— salt and black pepper

Fortifying salad

— 1 medium head white
   cauliflower (about 1 lb/500 g)
— 1 medium head Romanesco
   (about 1 lb/500 g)

For the dressing
— 7 tablespoons (100 ml)
   olive oil
— 2 tablespoons lemon juice
— salt and pepper

For the salad
— 3½ oz (100 g) pitted
   black olives
— 3½ oz (100 g) pitted
   green olives
— 4 tablespoons capers
— 6–7 anchovy fillets, chopped
— 1 pickled red pepper, cut
   into strips

This is a typical Christmas Eve dish in Naples and is termed "fortifying" as it is served to make a meal without meat—once compulsory according to the rules of the Catholic church—more substantial.

Preparation time: 30 minutes
Cooking time: 15 minutes
Serves 4

In separate pans of lightly salted boiling water, cook the whole heads of green and white cauliflower until crisp tender. When cool enough to handle, divide into florets.

To make the dressing: Whisk the oil in a small bowl with the lemon juice and salt and pepper to taste.

To assemble the salad: Arrange the florets in a large salad bowl, alternating the white ones with the green. Add the olives, capers, anchovies, and pickled pepper strips. Pour the dressing over everything and stir gently to avoid breaking up the cauliflower. (This salad can be prepared in advance and kept in the fridge. Remove it 30 minutes before serving to come back to room temperature.)

PIZZA NAPOLETANA

Preparation time: 25 minutes + 35 minutes rising
Cooking time: 20 minutes
Makes 2 small pizzas or 1 large pizza

Make the pizza dough, roll out, and line the pan(s) as directed in the dough recipe. Cover with a kitchen towel and let rest for 20 minutes.

Preheat the oven to 475°F (250°C/Gas Mark 9).

To make the topping: Spread the tomatoes evenly over the surface of the dough and crush any large pieces with a fork or by hand. Top with the garlic and salt and drizzle generously with olive oil. Bake for 10 minutes. Remove from the oven, sprinkle with oregano and bake until the crust is golden brown and crisp, 8–10 minutes. Serve warm.

Neapolitan pizza

— Pizza Dough (page 265)

For the topping
— 1 can (28 oz/795 g)
   San Marzano tomatoes,
   drained and seeded
— 2 cloves garlic, thinly sliced
— pinch of salt
— olive oil, for drizzling
— dried oregano, for sprinkling

PIZZA

Naples is the birthplace of pizza, and Neapolitans value and prize their role in culinary history with this global phenomenon of a dish. Pizza can be found in abundance all over Campania. Associazione Verace Pizza Napoletana is an association that was created to authenticate and ensure that Neapolitan institutions adhere to the correct guidelines and recipes for creating pizza.

Pizzas are baked in domed wood-burning ovens made of stone or brick. The pizza is baked right on the stone, not in a pizza pan; and the yeasted dough puffs and bubbles in the high heat, charring at the edges to give the pie a complex flavor.

The word "pizza" comes from the Romans and the Latin word *pinsa*, a sort of flat bread. Some believe the focaccia was the precursor to pizza. At the end of the eighteenth century, *co a pummarola 'ncoppa* (Neapolitan for "tomato sauce on top") began to spread throughout the city and pizza was exclusively sold as street food by traveling pizza vendors with small ovens. The first real pizzeria, Port'Alba, opened its doors in 1830.

In 1889, King Umberto I and Queen Margherita, curious about pizza, invited the pizza maker Don Raffaele and his wife, Pasqualina, to the kitchens of the Capodimonte palace. The queen's favorite became known as Pizza Margherita. The colors of the pie were also those of Italy's flag.

Pizzerias traditionally only serve two types of pizza: the *marinara*, a saucier pie, consists of a simple tomato sauce made from San Marzano tomatoes, garlic, oregano, and olive oil; and the Margherita, made with the same tomato sauce, basil, fior di latte (cow's milk mozzarella) or mozzarella di bufala for the purists, drizzled with olive oil.

Pages 72—73:
The region's economy is heavily reliant on agriculture.

Master pizza makers are known for their ability to pat out the dough, deftly throw it in the air, catch it, and throw it again.

BABÀ

Rum baba

For the dough
— 2 envelopes (¼ oz/7 g each)
   active dry yeast
— ¼ cup (50 ml) warm milk
— 2 tablespoons plus a pinch
   of granulated sugar
— 5 eggs
— 2 cups (250 g) all-purpose
   (plain) flour
— pinch of salt
— 9 tablespoons (4½ oz/125 g)
   butter, at room temperature

For the fruit
— 4–5 tablespoons raisins
— 8 prunes, halved
— 1 cup (250 ml) light rum
— 2 apples, peeled, cored,
   and cut into 8 wedges
— 3 pears, peeled, cored,
   and cut into 6 pieces
— 1½ cups (375 ml) water
— 3 tablespoons
   granulated sugar
— grated zest of ½ lemon

For the syrup
— 2 cups (200 g)
   granulated sugar
— 2 cups (450 ml) water →

Preparation time: 1 hour 30 minutes
+ 1 hour 30 minutes rising
Cooking time: 55 minutes
Makes 20

To make the dough: Dissolve the yeast in a glass with 2 tablespoons milk and a pinch of the sugar and set aside for 10 minutes. In a bowl, beat together 3 of the eggs.

Pile the flour on a work surface and make a well in the center. Add the salt, yeast mixture, beaten eggs, 2 tablespoons sugar, and half the softened butter. Pour in the remaining milk and knead together vigorously. Add the remaining 2 eggs and butter and knead the dough until it comes away from the work surface. Transfer the dough to a buttered bowl, cover with plastic wrap (clingfilm) and let rise in a warm place for about 1 hour 30 minutes.

Butter and flour 20 baba molds (or a tube pan or savarin mold with a capacity of 10–12 cups/2.5– 3 liters). With a wooden spoon, gently transfer the dough (which will be very soft) to the pan(s). Cover and let rise in a warm place until the dough reaches the top rim of the pan(s).

To prepare the fruit: Combine the raisins and prunes in a bowl, add enough rum to barely cover, and leave to soften thoroughly, about 15 minutes. Drain well.

Combine the apples, pears, and drained raisins and prunes in a large saucepan. Add the water, remaining rum, sugar, and lemon zest and cook over medium heat until the apples and pears are tender, about 20 minutes. Remove from the heat and let the fruit cool in the syrup.

— grated zest of ½ lemon
— 3½ tablespoons (50 ml) lemon juice
— 1¼ cups (300 ml) light rum

For serving
— 2 tablespoons apricot jam
— 2 tablespoons rum

Meanwhile, preheat the oven to 425°F (220°C/Gas Mark 7).

Place the babas in the oven and bake for 15 minutes, then reduce the temperature to 375°F (190°C/Gas Mark 5) and continue baking until golden brown and a toothpick comes out clean, 15–20 minutes.

Meanwhile, to prepare the syrup: Combine the sugar and water in a saucepan and cook until the sugar has dissolved. Remove from the heat, wait a few minutes, then add the lemon zest, lemon juice, and rum. Remove the baba(s) from the pan(s), let stand 5 minutes, then return to the pan(s), prick with a skewer and gradually pour the hot syrup over the baba(s) a little at a time, waiting until it has been fully absorbed before adding more: The baba(s) should absorb all of the syrup, but set aside a small amount for garnish later.

Stir the apricot jam and rum together. To serve, turn the rum babas out onto a serving dish, brush with a layer of the jam, and garnish with the cooked fruit. Serve the babas with more syrup on the side.

BABÀ

Rum baba, or *babà*, is a soft, puffy, yeasted cake, soaked in rum syrup. It is so popular in Campania, particularly Naples, that a compliment from a Neapolitan can be "*si nu' babba*," which is translated to "you are a baba."

Rum baba originated in France in the eighteenth century, and was invented by Stanislaw Leszczynski, twice the King of Poland, Duke of Lorraine, and father-in-law of Louis XV. Originally the dough was risen three times and kneaded at length to obtain a light and airy cake. It was filled with raisins from Corinth and Smyrna and was yellow on account of saffron. Legend has it that the saffron's fragrance reminded Leszczynski of his time in prison in Turkey. As an homage to *One Thousand and One Nights*, he called his cake the sweet Ali Baba. Baba came to Naples after the unification of Italy and no longer contains raisins or saffron.

Another legend states that Leszczynski enjoyed *Kugelhopf*, an Alsatian cake. Tired of the traditional Madeira used to flavor the dough, he dipped the cake in Marsala, and the original baba was born. The court's pastry chef then opened a shop in Paris a few years later, soaking this cake in rum. Chefs who worked for royal Neapolitan families brought the cake from Paris to Naples. Baba was mentioned in the first Italian cookbook, written by Angeletti, in 1836.

Whatever the origin may be, this ubiquitous treat is supremely popular in Naples. It can be prepared at home, but it's usually reserved for holidays because of the lengthy baking process, and every *pasticceria* will have a selection of babas. Babas can be served with additional rum or limoncello syrup and alongside fruit soaked in rum and garnished with whipped cream or pastry cream.

Page 83:
Piazza San Domenico Maggiore is one of the city's most important centers.

Babas are ubiquitous in regional pastry shops. Several sizes exist: larger cakes and smaller mushroom-shaped versions, originally referred to as "walking cakes."

COVIGLIE AL CIOCCOLATO

In Naples, chocolate mousse is generally served in special cups of silver-plated metal.

Preparation time: 45 minutes
Cooking time: 15 minutes
Serves 8–10

Break the chocolate into pieces and melt in a double boiler.

Beat the egg yolks with the sugar in a bowl until smooth and foamy, then add the rum and the melted chocolate.

Whip the cream until stiff peaks form.

Whip the egg whites with the lemon juice until stiff peaks form, about 5 minutes.

Fold the whipped cream very carefully into the chocolate mixture. Then fold in the egg whites. Divide the mixture among small glasses or ramekins, seal with plastic wrap and store in the freezer for a week at most. Remove from the freezer 20 minutes before serving.

Chocolate mousse

— 8 oz (225 g) semisweet or bittersweet chocolate (preferably 70% cacao)
— 4 egg yolks
— 6–8 tablespoons (80–100 g) granulated sugar (depending on the type of chocolate)
— 2 tablespoons light rum
— 1½ cups (350 ml) heavy (double) cream, chilled
— 3 egg whites, at room temperature
— 1 teaspoon lemon juice

COFFEE

The coffee drinking ritual has existed throughout Italy since the 1500s. Coffee, or *caffè*, originally was exotic and only available to the upper classes. In the nineteenth century, street sellers, *caffettiere*, appeared, making coffee available to the masses. These sellers carried roasted coffee beans, spreading an irresistible smell of coffee throughout the streets of Campania.

Naples is the birthplace of the espresso machine and the resulting popularity of coffee bars that ensued. Neapolitans stop at coffee bars several times a day, beginning with a milky coffee at breakfast. They often stop in for an afternoon jolt of espresso and then have another espresso, acting as a digestive, after dinner.

An Italian coffee bar has many customs. It is usual to drink coffee first, then pay. Most customers drink standing up at the counter. A uniquely Neapolitan tradition that gained popularity during World War II is *caffè sospeso*, or "suspended coffee." A customer pays in advance for a cup of coffee to be given to someone else who is unable to buy a cup of coffee due to financial hardship, but sometimes for other reasons. This small act of kindness has gained momentum throughout Europe and experienced a resurgence in the past couple of years.

The unparalleled taste of Campanian coffee is credited to many things: the original Neapolitan espresso machine, *machinetta napoletana*, which is fitted with a paper cone on the spout to prevent any fragrance from disappearing into the air; the coffee beans; and even the water. Naples' favorite sweets such as *babà* (page 80), *torta caprese alle noci* (page 93), or *sfogliatelle frolle* (page 213) would not be complete without the strong bite of a cup of espresso.

Page 86:
The Certosa di San Martino can be spotted from the narrow streets below. The former monastery complex sits beside the Castel Sant'Elmo.

Page 87:
The thirteenth-century Castel Nuovo, or New Castle, was founded by Charles I (also known as Charles of Anjou), king of Naples and Sicily. The castle is known locally as the Maschio Angioino, or Angevin Keep.

Coffee roasters and pastry shops in Naples are commonly found in the same vicinity.

TORTA CAPRESE ALLE NOCI

Preparation time: 40 minutes
Cooking time: 1 hour
Serves 8–10

Capri walnut cake

— 7 oz (200 g) dark chocolate
  (70% cacao), chopped
— 8 eggs, separated
— 1 tablespoon lemon juice
— 18 tablespoons (9 oz/250 g)
  butter, at room temperature
— 1¼ cups (250 g)
  granulated sugar
— 11 oz (300 g) walnuts
  or almonds, chopped
— Powdered (icing) sugar,
  for serving

Preheat the oven to 350°F (180°C/Gas Mark 4).
Line the bottom of a 10½-inch (26 cm) cake pan with
a round of parchment paper and grease and flour the
sides of the pan.

Melt the chocolate in a double boiler. (Alternatively,
microwave the chocolate in a microwave-safe bowl
in 30-second increments, stirring after each, until
melted.) Remove from the heat and let cool.

Beat the egg whites with the lemon juice until stiff
peaks form, about 5 minutes.

Beat the butter and granulated sugar in a bowl until
light and fluffy, 2–3 minutes. Mix in the egg yolks,
walnuts, and cooled chocolate, and mix together
thoroughly. Fold in the whipped egg whites.

Pour the batter into the prepared pan and bake for
1 hour. Cover the top of the cake toward the end
of the cooking time, if necessary. Allow to cool and
transfer the cake to a serving dish and sprinkle the
top with powdered sugar.

TORTA CAPRESE ALLE NOCI

The Capri walnut cake, or *torta caprese alle noci*, is a traditional walnut or almond chocolate cake invented on the island of Capri, located at the southern end of the Gulf of Naples. Several variations exist, but the flourless cake is made with nuts (finely chopped or ground into a flour) and whipped egg whites and yolks. Occasionally a splash of liquor is added. Sometimes decorated with a stencil, the cake is typically finished with a dusting of powdered (icing) sugar.

Several legends surround the creation of this decadent and moist cake. It's possibly a relative of the Austrian Sachertorte. Or it might be the result of a baker's accidental recipe substitution—a heavenly mistake. Primarily created for tourists on Capri, it became a popular mainstay delicacy of tearooms and pastry shops.

The sweet cake is traditionally served with glasses of chilled limoncello, another regional favorite unique to Capri.

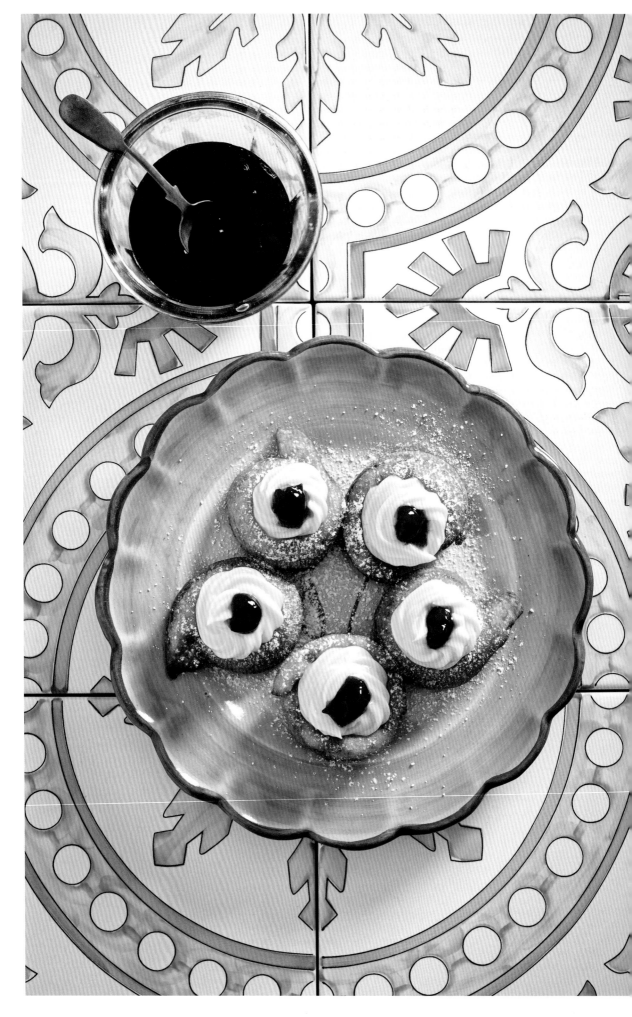

ZEPPOLE NAPOLETANE

Zeppole are one of the pastries traditionally made for the feast of Saint Joseph. In Campania, they are ring-shaped and garnished with cream and a cherry.

Preparation time: 45 minutes
Cooking time: 1 hour
Makes 10–12 doughnuts

Combine the water, butter, and salt in a saucepan and bring almost to a boil, or until the butter is melted. Remove the pan from the heat and add the flour all at once. Stir well with a wooden spoon, return the pan to medium-high heat, and continue to stir vigorously until the mixture pulls away from the sides of the pan. Pour the mixture into a bowl and leave to cool, about 5 minutes. Then beat in the eggs, one at a time. Beat in the lemon zest. Transfer the mixture to a pastry bag with round tip.

Pour enough oil to come halfway up the sides of a medium Dutch oven (casserole) or heavy-bottomed pot. Heat over medium-high heat until it reaches 350°F (180°C). Pipe 2 tablespoons of batter onto a metal slotted spoon, creating a round, ball-like shape. Drop the spoon in the hot oil so that the doughnut rolls off the spoon. Repeat, frying 4 doughnuts at a time, turning the doughnuts over several times until they are golden brown, 1–2 minutes per side. Remove and drain on a plate lined with paper towels.

Serve warm or at room temperature. Sprinkle with powdered sugar or dollop a spoonful of jam or pastry cream into the middle of the doughnut.

Neapolitan doughnuts

— 1 cup (250 ml) water
— 6 tablespoons (3 oz/80 g) butter or lard
— pinch of salt
— 1¾ cups (225 g) all-purpose (plain) flour, sifted
— 6 eggs
— grated zest of 1 lemon
— canola oil, for deep-frying

For serving
— powdered (icing) sugar
— chery jam
— pastry cream

PASTIERA NAPOLETANA

Pastiera napoletana, an Easter delicacy, has both Roman and Greek provenances. It is said that the cheesecake-like dessert comes from baptism ceremony breads made with milk and honey during Constantine's reign. The cake was said to symbolize resurrection and new life, common themes during Easter. Another legend is of locals honoring the siren Parenope—who emerged from the Gulf of Naples every spring—with offerings of the traditional *pastiera* ingredients. She then took the ingredients to the gods under the sea, who mixed them together to create *pastiera napoletana*. Most likely, the cake was created in a Neapolitan convent.

While *pastiera* is a common accompaniment to coffee, the lengthy baking process marks it as a festive treat, meant to be savored. For it to be ready in time for an Easter feast, the cake had to be made before Maundy Thursday or Good Friday because of the lengthy cooking and cooling times.

These days, *pastiera* is made with precooked grain, or *grano cotto*, a jarred product created for the sole purpose of making *pastiera*. (Extremely rare outside of Italy, cooked pearl barley or wheat berries can be substituted.) The cooked grain is reheated slowly in milk until creamy and plump. It is this ingredient that creates *pastiera's* unique personality.

The creamy wheat is then combined with eggs, ricotta, orange blossom water, cinnamon, and vanilla to make a filling. Candied citron or *zucca candita*, candied pumpkin, is added for texture and sweetness. The filling is placed in a pastry crust and lattice strips of dough are woven over the top. The cake is baked and then cooled for at least a day. Modern versions of this cake use pastry cream in the filling, creating a softer, fluffier texture.

Café tables line the streets of Naples.

PASTIERA NAPOLETANA

Preparation time: 1 hour 15 minutes + 12 hours chilling
Cooking time: 1 hour 30 minutes
Serves 12

To make the filling: Combine the barley, milk,
2½ tablespoons of the sugar, the salt, and zest of ½
a lemon and cook slowly until the grains are almost
dry, yet tender, stirring often to prevent it sticking
to the pan, about 20 minutes. Remove from the heat
and cool.

While the barley is cooking, whisk the egg whites
with the lemon juice until stiff peaks form. Set aside.

Cream the ricotta with the remaining sugar in a bowl,
add the egg yolks, candied citron, candied pumpkin,
orange blossom water, remaining lemon zest, and the
cooled barley mixture. Mix until combined. Gently
fold in the egg whites until combined.

Preheat the oven to 325°F (170°C/Gas Mark 3).
Grease and flour a 12-inch (30 cm) cake pan.

To prepare the pastry: Pile the flour on a work suface
and make a well in the center. Add the sugar, butter or
lard, egg yolks, and orange zest, kneading the dough
until it becomes smooth and even. Cut off one-quarter
of the pastry and set aside. Roll out the remaining
pastry to a 15-inch (38 cm) round and carefully fit it
into the prepared pan, allowing it to come up the sides
of the pan. Trim any excess dough.

Fill the pastry with the ricotta mixture. Roll out
the reserved pastry to a 15-inch (38 cm) round and cut
into 6 thick strips. Form the strips into a lattice. Trim
any excess dough and crimp the edges to seal the pastry.

Bake for 1 hour 30 minutes. Cool and refrigerate for
at least 12 hours before serving.

Neapolitan pastiera

For the filling
— 2⅔ cups (420 g) cooked pearl
  barley, cooled
— 2¼ cups (500 ml) whole milk
— 1⅓ cups (280 g) granulated
  sugar
— pinch of salt
— grated zest of 1½ lemons
— 3 egg whites
— 1 teaspoon lemon juice
— 2 cups (1 lb 2 oz/500 g)
  fresh ricotta cheese
— 5 egg yolks
— 3 oz (70 g) candied citron,
  diced (about ¾ cup)
— 3 oz (70 g) candied pumpkin
  or dried apricots, diced
  (about ¾ cup)
— 1 teaspoon orange
  blossom water

For the pastry
— 3¾ cups (500 g) all-purpose
  (plain) flour
— 1 cup (200 g) granulated
  sugar
— 18 tablespoons (9 oz/250 g)
  butter or lard, at room
  temperature
— 5 egg yolks
— grated zest of 1 orange

VESUVIAN APRICOTS

Campania is the primary producer of Italian apricots and well known for the celebrated Vesuvius apricots, which are awarded PGI status (protected geographical indication), meaning they are grown according to traditional standards. Trees grow on the slopes of Monte Somma, a collapsed volcano out of which rises Mt. Vesuvius. The mineral-rich and fertile soil, and the excellent, mild climate, create perfect growing conditions for apricots. Intensely flavored, aromatic, with a rich, orange hue flecked with red, the apricots have a brief season from June to July, thus contributing to their rarity. The tree-ripened fruit is so tender that it must be picked by hand.

Apricots, or Vesuvian apricots, are the most popular fruit in the area surrounding Mt. Vesuvius. However, about seventy or more varieties exist, and are differentiated by size, aroma, skin texture, and flavor. Flavor can vary intensely in scale from sweet to sour. Representing a range, Pellecchiella and Monaco varieties are known as the sweetest, and Cafona or Vitillo varieties are known as bitter.

Some apricots go to local markets to be eaten as whole fruit, but the majority of the harvest goes to making juice, pastes, candied fruit, and jams.

Pages 104—105:
A bird's-eye view of the city's labyrinth of ancient Roman streets.

CASERTA

CASERTA

North of Naples, Caserta is located on the plain at the foot of Campania's Apennine mountain range. This undiscovered subdued region is often times forgotten, due to its distance from the primary Naples train line and proximity to the more exciting Amalfi Coast. While the modern town was bombed heavily in World War II, Casertavecchia, a medieval hamlet, boasts original paving, stone archways, and endless preserved details, as well as a twelfth-century cathedral in Norman-Arab style and an eleventh-century Norman castle.

The establishment of Caserta is often debated and unknown as to which group to give paternity: the Samnites, Longobards, or Romans. The royal Bourbon family chose Caserta as the site of their new palace in the eighteenth century for its geographic location. The town grew to support the needs of the royal palace. Toward the end of World War II, the palace hosted the Supreme Allied Commander, and was the site where the German forces eventually surrendered.

Reggia di Caserta, Royal Palace of Caserta, was designed by the Baroque architect Luigi Vanvitelli. The royal palace was constructed over twenty years and was built with the best possible craftsmanship and materials and was most likely the largest Italian building built at the time. This sumptuous and grand Italian palace is a keystone of Campania's tourist industry. The rectangular building, which hosts a spectacular royal staircase, is divided into quarters with multiple courtyards. The splendid royal apartments and the English gardens, which include fountains, ponds, and statues, are a triumph that should not be missed.

Caserta is prized for its craftsmanship. There is a lengthy history of silkworm farms and weaving factories. The region is home to abundant chestnut forests, vineyards, and olive groves. Casertano pigs roam

Page 106:
A heavily laden "Ape" van on its way to the market is a common sight in Caserta.

Lavish frescoes adorn the ceilings of the Reggia di Caserta.

Page 110:
One of the two lion statues that anchor the grand marble staircase of the Reggia di Caserta.

Page 111:
The grandiose palace measures over 484,376 square feet (45,000 sq m).

freely and pork and wild boar are featured ingredients in dishes such as roast pork, sausages, wild boar with fresh pasta, and grilled baby pig. Caserta is known for its *salsiccia*, a sausage seasoned in terra-cotta vases. Well known for the *capuanella* artichoke, Caserta is also noted for its preeminent mozzarella di bufala production. Since ancient times, Italian water buffalo have been bred and roam the countryside of Caserta. Besides the famously silky and fresh DOC mozzarella, buffalo milk is also used to make other cheeses such as burrata, smoked provola, and ricotta.

Watermelons, cantaloupes, and canary melons at a roadside stand.

TARALLI AL FINOCCHIETTO

Preparation time: 1 hour + 2 hours rising
Cooking time: 1 hour 15 minutes
Makes 20

Preheat the oven to 400°F (200°C/Gas Mark 6).
Line two baking sheets with parchment paper.

Combine the yeast, sugar, and a few tablespoons of
the warm water in a bowl. Set aside for a few minutes.

Pile the flour on a work surface and make a well in
the center. Sprinkle the salt into the well and the
lard, almonds, fennel seeds, pepper, and yeast mixture.
Knead, adding the remaining warm water to obtain
a smooth dough. Transfer to a bowl coated with
oil, cover, and let rise in a warm place until doubled
in volume, about 2 hours.

Divide the dough into 4 portions and roll each into a
long rope about 20 inches (50 cm) long. Cut crosswise
into 4-inch (10 cm) lengths. Cross the two ends of the
pieces to form a ring, pressing the ends firmly to seal.

Evenly space the taralli on the prepared baking sheets.
Bake for about 15 minutes. Turn off the oven and, with
the door slightly ajar, leave the taralli in the oven for
1 hour or until they are completely dry and crunchy.

Fennel-flavored
taralli

— 2 envelopes (¼ oz/7 g each)
   active dry yeast
— pinch of granulated sugar
— ¾ cup plus 2 tablespoons
   (200 ml) warm water
— 3¾ cups (500 g) all-purpose
   (plain) flour
— 1 tablespoon salt
— 10 tablespoons (5 oz/150 g)
   lard or butter, at room
   temperature
— 2 cups (7 oz/200 g) coarsely
   chopped almonds
— 2 teaspoons fennel seeds
— pinch of pepper
— olive oil, for brushing

TARALLI

Taralli, or savory fennel crackers, are traditionally
eaten with slices of salami. The word *taralli* refers to
the street sellers who used to sell them in Megellina,
a fishing port in the city of Naples. These street sellers
no longer exist, but taralli are some of Campania's
first versions of street foods, meant to be enjoyed at sea
or on a walk along the harbor. Shaped into rings and
flavored with ingredients such as fennel seeds, almonds,
lard, and occasionally wine, the yeasted dough can also
be sweetened with a dusting of powdered (icing) sugar.

Legend states that bakers created these savory treats
in the seventeenth century from leftover bread dough
and enhanced them with lard and pepper so as not
to waste the dough.

Similar to a crunchy cracker or breadstick, they can
be dunked in wine and are a popular tavern snack.
There are larger and smaller versions of taralli, each
made to a specific and standard measurement. They
can be deep-fried, baked, or boiled in water before
being baked, and tend to last for several months.

Bags of taralli can be found
throughout the region.

CAPRESE DI MOZZARELLA
DI BUFALA

Preparation time: 20 minutes
Serves 4

*Mozzarella and
tomato salad*

Slice the tomatoes and remove the seeds. Cut the
mozzarella into ⅛-inch (3 mm) slices. On a serving
dish, alternate the tomato and mozzarella slices in
concentric circles. Sprinkle with the basil leaves,
drizzle with oil, and season with salt. Keep cool until
ready to serve.

— 3–4 tomatoes
— 11 oz (300 g)
   buffalo mozzarella
— ¼ cup (6 g) basil leaves
— olive oil, for drizzing
— salt

BUFFALO MOZZARELLA

Mozzarella di bufala is a porcelain-white fresh cheese made exclusively in Campania from the milk of native Italian water buffalos that roam the plains of Caserta and Salerno. This silky and dense cheese is protected by the Consortium for the Protection of Buffalo Mozzarella, founded in 1981. There are about two hundred producers, and they are subjected to inspections from the Consortium, which monitor everything from breeding processes to dairy organization and selling practices. Buffalo mozzarella holds a DOC (controlled designation of origin) status, which means, as of 1993, that it may only be produced by a traditional recipe in certain areas, including Campania. The cheese has been awarded several trademarks and Protected Geographical Status or PDO, which the product gained in 1996.

The history of the region's black water buffalo, with long sharp horns and powerful hooves, is shrouded. Many credit the Asian buffalo, brought to Italy in the Middle Ages. Others believe buffalos were brought to Italy by the Normans, or by pilgrims and crusaders. Buffalo mozzarella was prevalent throughout the second half of the eighteenth century, but production halted after the herds were brutally slaughtered during World War II. However, production was reestablished after the armistice.

Cow's milk can also be made into mozzarella, but mozzarella di bufala is considered superior in Campania as the buffalo milk is richer with increased levels of protein, fat, and minerals. The buffalos produce less milk per day than cows, making the milk more of a rarity. Fior di latte, which means flower of milk, is another term for cow's milk mozzarella. This cheese is a member of the *pasta filata* family, "spun paste," which means that after curdling the raw milk with whey, the resulting curds are stretched in hot water with a stick-like ladle. The expert hands of the

Buffalo mozzarella is submerged in whey to preserve its freshness.

The provinces of Caserta and Salerno account for around 90 percent of certified production of buffalo mozzarella in the entire PDO (protected geographical status) area.

cheesemaker then skillfully chop off a portion —the verb in Italian is *mozzare*, hence the name mozzarella—which then is shaped into a ball. The cheese is plunged into warm brine for a few hours. Instead of the telltale, elastic globes of mozzarella, smaller balls or *bocconcini* can also be formed or the mozzarella can be plaited into larger, knotted shapes; however, the larger shapes must be under 1¾ pounds (800 g) to be considered buffalo mozzarella. Over 1 gallon (4 liters) of fresh buffalo milk are needed to produce 2¼ pounds (1 kg) of mozzarella.

Best served fresh and at room temperature, this slightly tangy and sweet cheese lends its milky note to *pizza Margherita* (page 191), where torn or grated bits of cheese easily melt and commingle with fresh tomato sauce. *Caprese di mozzarella di bufala* (page 119), Mozzarella and Tomato Salad, is an antipasto dish of sliced tomatoes, buffalo mozzarella, and basil. Garnished with salt and olive oil, legend states that the salad is meant to resemble the Italian flag, and features fresh Campanian ingredients at their absolute best. The origin of the salad is not exactly known, but it first appeared on the menu at Hotel Quisisana in Capri in 1924.

Pages 124–125:
Summer produce makes its way to the local markets.

CALZONCINI 'MBOTTONATI

Preparation time: 45 minutes + 1 hour rising
Cooking time: 30 minutes
Makes 9

To make the dough: In a bowl, add the yeast, sugar, and 2 tablespoons of the warm milk and stir until dissolved. Let sit for 10–15 minutes.

Pile the flour on a work surface and create a well in the center. Add the yeast mixture, the remaining milk, and salt to the flour and knead by hand to obtain a smooth and even dough, about 2 minutes. Add more milk or water, if needed.

To make the filling: Beat the ricotta in a bowl until smooth. Add the provolone, pancetta, egg, and salt and mix well.

Divide the dough in half and roll out each portion to a 12-inch (30 cm) round. Over one of the rounds, distribute nine 3–4 tablespoon balls of filling, evenly spaced, and cover with the second round of the dough, stretching it over the filling and sealing the edges. Use a 3-inch (7.5 cm) glass or round cutter to cut out the *calzoncini*. Seal any loose edges. Line up the *calzoncini* on a lightly floured cloth and let rise in a warm place for at least 1 hour.

Pour enough oil into a medium Dutch oven (casserole) or heavy-bottomed pot to come halfway up the sides. Heat over medium–high heat to 350°F (180°C). Use a slotted spoon to lower half the *calzoncini* into the oil. Be careful as the oil will bubble up. Let them fry, flipping them halfway through, until the seams begin to turn golden brown, 3–4 minutes. Remove from the oil with the slotted spoon and drain on a plate lined with paper towels. Allow the oil to come back up to 350°F (180°C) and fry the remaining batch. Serve hot.

For the dough
— ¼ oz (7 g) active dry yeast
— pinch of granulated sugar
— ¾ cup (180 ml) warm
  milk or water, as needed
— 2⅓ cups (300 g) all-purpose
  (plain) flour
— pinch of salt

For the filling
— 1¼ cups (11 oz/300 g) ricotta
  cheese
— 3 oz (80 g) provolone
  cheese, grated
— 3½ oz (100 g)
  pancetta, minced
— 1 egg
— pinch of salt

— canola oil, for deep-frying

Lasagna with artichokes

For the béchamel
— 3 tablespoons (2 oz/28 g) unsalted butter
— 3 tablespoons (25g) all-purpose (plain) flour
— pinch of salt
— 2 cups (475 ml) milk

For the pasta
— 2¾ cups (300 g) 00 flour
— 3 eggs
— 2 tablespoons olive oil

For the filling
— 12 baby or 6 large artichokes (or 28 oz/800 g canned water-packed artichoke hearts, drained)
— 6 tablespoons (3 oz/80 g) butter
— 3½ oz (100 g) Parmesan cheese, grated (about 1 cup)
— 1⅔ cups (13 oz/375 g) ricotta cheese, drained
— 3.5 oz (110 g) cooked ham, chopped
— generous ⅔ cup (150 ml) heavy (double) cream
— salt and pepper

Preparation time: 1 hour
Cooking time: 1 hour 45 minutes
Serves 8

To make the béchamel: Heat the butter in a medium saucepan over medium heat until melted. Whisk in the flour and salt and cook for 2 minutes. Slowly pour in the milk, whisking the entire time, until combined. Whisking constantly, bring the mixture to a boil and simmer until thick enough to coat the back of a spoon, 3–5 minutes. Remove from the heat and let cool.

To make the pasta: Pile the flour on a work surface and create a well in the center. Add the eggs. Blend in a little flour at a time, pour in 1 tablespoon of the oil and knead the mixture until smooth and elastic, about 2 minutes. Divide the dough into 4 pieces and flatten into rounds. Using a pasta machine, starting on the thickest setting, run 1 round of dough through each setting twice, until smooth and translucent. Repeat until all the dough is rolled out into sheets. Cut each sheet into 12-inch (30 cm) long pieces and set aside. (Alternatively, roll out the rounds of dough using a rolling pin until translucent.)

Bring a large pot of salted water to a boil and add the remaining 1 tablespoon oil. Boil a batch of 4–5 noodles at a time until al dente, 2–3 minutes. Drain and dry on a kitchen towel. Repeat until all the noodles are cooked. Set aside.

To prepare the filling: Bring a pot of water to a boil. Pull off all the leaves of the artichokes. Use a paring knife and vegetable peeler to remove any tough or dark bits of skin around the base, stem, and heart. Slice each heart in half and use a spoon to remove the choke. Blanch the hearts for a few minutes then plunge into cold water to stop the cooking process. (No need to blanch canned artichokes, if using.) Drain.

Heat 2 tablespoons of the butter in a frying pan set over medium-high heat. Add the artichokes and sauté until golden brown, about 10 minutes.

While the artichokes are cooking, mix the cooled béchamel with half the grated Parmesan in a bowl. Add the ricotta, ham, and cream. Stir the mixture until smooth, add salt and pepper, and taste for seasoning.

Preheat the oven to 350°F (180°C/Gas Mark 4). Grease a 9 x 13-inch (23 x 33 cm) baking dish and place on top of a baking sheet.

Arrange 3 cooked lasagna noodles on the bottom of the prepared pan, pour over half of the ricotta mixture, then add another layer of 3 noodles, all of the artichokes, 3 more noodles, the remaining ricotta mixture, and end with the remaining 3 noodles. Sprinkle the top layer with the remaining Parmesan. Cube the remaining 4 tablespoons butter and dot over the lasagna. Cover with foil and bake for 45 minutes. Remove from the oven and let rest for 15 minutes before serving.

ARTICHOKES

Page 131:
The Reggia di Caserta was built to rival the courts of Paris, London, and Madrid.

Artichokes are an edible variety of a thistle species developed in the Mediterranean and consumed in ancient times by Greeks and Romans. Southern Italy grows almost fifty percent of artichokes worldwide, including several other specialty varieties such as the tiny purple Anzio, oval Siena, sweet Mercury, large Chianti, and King.

Another prized member of the species, grown only in Campania, includes the *carciofo capuanella*. The name refers to the town of Capua in Caserta, a region known for its artichoke crops. Capuanella artichokes are ready for harvest toward the beginning of spring. This specimen is medium in size and a brilliant, hunter green in color, but can also be found in a violet hue. The tight, tough leaves protect a tender heart with a spherical head.

Capuanella artichokes are traditionally roasted by fire, or slow-cooked in a pot, with holes on the bottom for draining, and then laid on hot coals. Often tossed simply with olive oil, parsley, and garlic before cooking, the intense scent of the cooking artichokes drifts throughout the villages and towns of Caserta. Artichokes can be trimmed, a time-consuming yet worthwhile process, which yields delicate and supple hearts, a contrast to the nutty and tangy flesh on the base of each leaf.

Used as a luscious and meatless filling for lasagna (page 128), stuffed with mozzarella and baked, topped on crostini, or used to fill or top pizzas, artichokes are a versatile yet exceptional ingredient. Throughout Italy artichokes are often served fried, stuffed, marinated, or as an antipasto with the hearts and leaves packed in oil.

The hunter green, or violet artichokes are typical cultivars of the region.

CHITARRA CON ZUCCA E MAZZANCOLLE

Chitarra pasta with pumpkin and shrimp

Preparation time: 30 minutes
Cooking time: 30 minutes
Serves 6

— 14 oz (400 g) pumpkin, peeled
— ¼ cup (50 ml) olive oil
— 1 clove garlic, peeled
    but whole
— 1½ lb (700 g) shell-on shrimp
    (prawns)
— ¼ cup (50 ml) dry white wine
— 1 tablespoon pink
    peppercorns
— 1 lb (500 g) spaghetti
    alla chitarra
— salt
— 2 tablespoons chopped
    parsley

Cut the pumpkin into long, thin strips to give them the same shape as spaghetti *alla chitarra*.

Heat the oil in a large frying pan. Add the garlic and brown. Remove and discard the garlic. Add the pumpkin and cook, stirring, over high heat for 5 minutes. Add the shrimp, stir, and after 5 minutes drizzle with the wine. When the wine has evaporated, reduce the heat and add the peppercorns.

Meanwhile, cook the spaghetti in a large pot of boiling salted water until al dente.

Drain the pasta, add it to the pan with the pumpkin and shrimp sauce, and gently toss. Transfer the pasta to a hot serving dish and sprinkle with the parsley. Serve hot.

FRIARIELLI

If Campania is identified by its arresting terraced lemon groves, it is also known for its fields of *friarielli*. A relative of *cimi di rapa*, or broccoli rabe, vibrant bright green *friarielli* is a cruciferous vegetable in the *Brassiaceae*, or mustard family. Its name translates literally to "turnip tops" and it is most likely related to a wild herb and the turnip, which grew in China or the Mediterranean. Common in Italian cuisine, the vegetable is known for its bitter and nutty taste.

Edible, tender leaves connect to green buds, which resemble broccoli heads, on which little, golden flowers oftentimes sprout. *Friarielli* is inexpensive and requires little effort to grow. Typically used as a side dish for pork (usually *salsiccia*, or sausage), *friarielli* is sautéed with olive oil, garlic, a pinch of crushed chili peppers, and seasoned simply with salt and pepper. This popular vegetable is also featured as a pizza topping or tangled with pasta. Oftentimes *friarielli* is served as a hearty, vegetable counterpoint alongside mozzarella di bufala or grilled scamorza cheese.

Vivid green *friarielli* on sale at a market in Campania.

Pages 138—139: Oblong, deep-purple eggplants (aubergines) grow in abundance in the summer months.

SPEZZATINO DI MAIALE

Preparation time: 20 minutes + 2 hours marinating
Cooking time: 20 minutes
Serves 6

Place the pork in a bowl and season with salt and pepper to taste and the fennel. Cover and let marinate for 2 hours.

Heat the oil in a saucepan over medium–high heat. Add the pancetta and the pork and brown slowly for 10 minutes, stirring often. Add the peppers and cook, stirring, for a few minutes. Remove from the heat and transfer to a serving dish. Serve hot.

Pork stew

— 2¼ lb (1 kg) pork (not too lean so that it stays tender), cut into cubes
— salt and pepper
— 2 tablespoons chopped fennel fronds
— 2–3 tablespoons olive oil
— 3½ oz (100 g) pancetta, diced
— 4 large pickled peppers, julienned

CASERTANO PIGS

Casertano pigs are an ancient and rare breed whose origin dates back at least to Pompeii and Herculaneum (based on paintings found at those sites). Though popular from ancient times, in the mid-twentieth century they quickly became more expensive than imported pigs. Casertano pigs roam freely in forested pastures throughout Caserta but are also found in Benevento. There is a producers' association, which was founded by ten breeders.

The slate gray pigs are a cross between the Avellino, Benevento, Caserta, and Salerno wild boars and the Spanish *pata negra*. In addition to their dark color, the pigs have short, thin legs, and are almost hairless. Their snouts, rectangular and narrow, enable the pigs to easily find acorns, hazelnuts, berries, and chestnuts as they roam. The pigs also have two wattles, *bargigli*, on the sides of their necks.

The pigs fatten well and the lean meat is marbled, creating tender pork with earthy flavors. The pigs produce an excellent lard, used often for pizza dough or *casatiello rustico* (page 207), a traditional Easter bread made with copious amounts of lard. The meat is best enjoyed transformed into *salsiccia* (sausage), cured meats, or by slow-cooking larger cuts of meat.

Two regional delicacies have been created from the Casertano pigs: *salame di maiale nero casertano,* salami from Casertano pigs, as well as a variety of sausage made with the pork, salt, spices, and white wine. Another specialty is *prosciutto di Pietraroja*, which is made in Benevento. The prosciutto is eaten raw, served in thin slices, and is only lightly smoked. Made from the hind legs of pigs slaughtered on warmer winter days, the lean part of the prosciutto is a dark red and the fat is bright and luminescent. This process and product is rare as only one man in the 1990s was still making *prosciutto di Pietraroja*.

With less hair than other breeds, the Casertano pig has been nicknamed *pelatello*, or little bald one.

TORTANO DEL MATESE

Preparation time: 30 minutes + 45 minutes rising
Cooking time: 1 hour
Serves 10–12

Dissolve the yeast and sugar in a small amount of the
warm water and mix with 2 tablespoons of the flour
to make a paste. Cover and set aside for 10–15 minutes.

Pile the remaining flour on a work surface and make
a well in the center. Stir the salt into the remaining
water and mix until the salt is dissolved. To the well
in the flour, add the lard, yeast mixture, and some
of the water mixture and knead to obtain a smooth
and elastic texture, 3–5 minutes. (Alternatively,
add the flour and ingredients to a stand mixer fitted
with the dough hook and knead until smooth,
3–5 minutes.)

Preheat the oven to 375°F (190°C/Gas Mark 5).
Line a large baking sheet with parchment paper.

To prepare the filling: Roll out the dough into a
rectangle about 7 x 5 inches (18 x 12 cm) and ⅓ inch
(1 cm) thick. Spread the salami, mortadella and
scamorza cheese over the dough, overlapping and
alternating these ingredients with the grated pecorino
and a pinch of black pepper, leaving a 1¼-inch
(3 cm) border. Roll up the dough like a jelly roll
(Swiss roll), placing the roll seam side down, and set
aside to rise in a warm place for 30 minutes.

Place the roll on the prepared baking sheet, seam
side down, and brush with oil. Bake for 1 hour.
Remove from the oven and let rest for 10 minutes.
Carefully slice the *tortano* with a serrated knife. Serve
warm or at room temperature.

Stuffed Easter bread

For the dough
— 2 envelopes (¼ oz/7 g each)
    active dry yeast
— 1 teaspoon granulated sugar
— 1¼ cups (295 ml)
    warm water
— 8 cups (1 kg) all-purpose
    (plain) flour
— 1¾ teaspoons salt
— 14 tablespoons (7 oz/200 g)
    lard or butter, at room
    temperature

For the filling
— 3½ oz (100 g) salami,
    thinly sliced
— 3½ oz (100 g) mortadella,
    thinly sliced
— 1 lb (450 g) scamorza or
    fresh mozzarella cheese,
    thinly sliced
— 1½ cups (3½ oz/100 g)
    grated pecorino cheese
— pepper

— olive oil, for brushing

CANASCIONE

Pizza with cheese and salami filling

For the dough
— 1 envelope (¼ oz/7 g)
   active dry yeast
— 1 teaspoon granulated sugar
— warm water
— 2⅓ cups (250 g) 00 flour
— 2 tablespoons olive oil
— ½ teaspoon salt

For the filling
— 3 eggs
— 1 cup (3½ oz/100 g) chopped
   caciotta or grated aged
   provolone
— 3 oz (80 g) salami, chopped
— pepper

— 1 egg, beaten

Canascione, also known as *pizza chiena* or "pizza with filling," has a number of versions of the filling with varying degrees of richness. The following recipe is the classic version, which includes eggs, cheese, and salami.

Preparation time: 25 minutes + 1 hour 15 minutes rising
Cooking time: 30 minutes
Serves 6–8

To make the dough: Combine the yeast, sugar, and a little warm water and stir to dissolve. Set aside for 10–15 minutes.

Pile the flour on a work surface and make a well in the center. Add the yeast mixture, oil, salt, and more warm water, as needed, and knead together to create a smooth and even dough. Form a ball, cover it with a kitchen towel and let rise in a warm place for 1 hour.

To make the filling: Beat the eggs in a bowl with the cheese, salami, and pepper to taste. Set aside.

Preheat the oven to 400°F (200°C/Gas Mark 6). Grease a 9–10½-inch (23–27 cm) cake pan.

Divide the dough into two portions, one slightly larger than the other. Roll the larger piece into a 12-inch (30 cm) round and carefully fit it into the prepared pan, allowing it to come up the sides of the pan. Trim any excess dough. Spread the filling into the cake pan without pressing down too much. Roll out the smaller piece into an 11-inch (28 cm) round and lay it over the filling. Trim any excess dough and crimp the edges to seal the pastry. Brush the surface with the beaten egg and prick the surface a few times with a skewer. Bake for 25–30 minutes. Serve warm.

III

SALERNO AND THE AMALFI COAST

SALERNO AND THE AMALFI COAST

The dramatic, sheer terrain of the Amalfi Coast is unlike anywhere else in the world. Breathtaking beaches hug rocky outcrops, interspersed with colorful harbors and coves. Villages, vineyards, and terrace gardens appear to grow directly out of cliffs. Beginning in Sorrento and ending in Amalfi, a thirty-mile (48 km) winding, narrow, and at times even dangerous coastal drive takes visitors by each famous resort town.

Tourists are treated to outstanding scenery, such as the medieval watchtowers along the coast, and excellent hiking and swimming. For a while, the region served as a seductive refuge to famous artists such as Wagner, Gore Vidal, and Picasso. Innumerable opportunities for inspiration exist, simply by walking the medieval towns and harbors, taking in the heavily citrus-scented air, and journeying the footpaths between coastal towns. Seafood dominates coastal cuisine and is usually featured with homemade pastas, tossed with sauces of clams or mussels. Seafood is also served fried in dishes such as *fritto misto* featuring calamari or shrimp.

Positano is the most famous and glamorous of the villages on the Amalfi Coast. High above the sea, the narrow pedestrian walkways and limited traffic give way to the staggering, steep sets of stairs and pebbled beaches. A quiet town, and at times insular, the village provides little to do except relax on beaches, eat, and admire the scenery punctuated by the colorful Mediterranean white, pink, and yellow houses. Positano, in addition to the small seaside village of Vietri sul Mare, are both known for their longstanding (since the fifteenth century) production of ceramics, which are created from Campania's famous mineral-rich clay. Designs draw heavily on the coast's inspiring and memorable color scheme of yellow, blue, and green.

By contrast, the quieter Ravello, also known for its ceramics, is not located by the sea, and instead perches

Page 148:
The crystalline waters of the Mediterranean entice bathers.

The coastline of the Amalfi Coast stretches for more than thirty miles (48 km) and is known for its warm, clear waters that attract Italian and international tourists alike.

Ceramic tiles adorn the walls and floors of this building in Vietri sul Mare.

precariously above the cliffs. It is worth visiting to see the grand villas and cliffside gardens, as well as Villa Rufolo, a Moorish and Norman style villa built in the thirteenth century, and Villa Cimbrone, which boasts spectacular views and gardens.

Though quiet today, the town of Amalfi was once a maritime republic, even competing with Venice, during the tenth and eleventh centuries. Amalfi controlled the luxury goods trade, transporting spices, perfumes, silks, and carpets around the Mediterranean, even as far as Byzantium. Amalfi was so important in its time that it held its own established rules of sea and minted its own coins. Besides trade, Amalfi was well known in the twelfth century for producing *bambagina*, thick handmade paper. As a result of a lethal plague and tsunami in the fourteenth century, Amalfi slid into the background of southern Italy. It was rediscovered as a tourist destination in the nineteenth century.

Surrounded by mountains and the most important harbor after Naples in Campania, Salerno's point of pride is a medieval town and cathedral, mostly intact after World War II bombing. Lungomare Trieste, which in Italian means "along the sea," is a seaside promenade along the Gulf of Salerno created in the 1950s. Lined with rare palm trees, this fine walkway is considered the most beautiful in Italy and is seen as a replica of the French Riviera. In the sixteenth century Salerno was the epicenter for culture, arts, and education. Ruled by the Spanish until the eighteenth century, this town was largely focused on textile production.

The quieter Cilento Coast, also a region of Salerno, boasts pristine water and a national park. Cilento's superior terroir is evidenced in its excellent wines, mozzarella di bufala, and olive oil production. The Greek temples of Paestum in the mountainous region of Cilento were founded in the sixth century BC and rediscovered in the eighteenth century; they are some of the best-preserved temples in Europe.

Pages 154—155:
Some hidden coves along the rocky coast are only accessible by boat.

COZZE GRATINATE

Mussels au gratin

— 3 lb 6 oz (1.5 kg)
    mussels, well scrubbed
— 2 cups (9 oz/250 g)
    breadcrumbs
— scant ½ cup (100 ml)
    olive oil, plus more for
    brushing
— 2 cloves garlic, minced
— 2 tablespoons capers,
    finely chopped
— 2 tablespoons chopped
    parsley
— salt and pepper

Preparation time: 45 minutes
Cooking time: 30 minutes
Serves 4–6

Preheat the oven to 375°F (190°C/Gas Mark 5).

In a large saucepan with 1 inch (2.5 cm) boiling water, steam the mussels, covered, until they open, 2 minutes. (Discard any mussels that do not open.) Set a sieve over a bowl, pour in the mussels and cooking juices. Set both aside.

Combine the breadcrumbs, oil, garlic, capers, and parsley in a bowl. Season with salt and pepper to taste. Pour in the strained cooking juices and toss gently to thoroughly moisten all the breadcrumbs, adding more breadcrumbs if the mixture is too wet.

Open up the mussel shells and discard the half that doesn't have the mussel in it. Line up the mussels in their half shells in an oven dish brushed with oil. Cover the mussels with the breadcrumb mixture and bake at for about 5 minutes. Serve hot.

CHESTNUTS

Page 158:
A peek of blue sea can
be spotted from up high.

Page 159:
Small plots of steeply
terraced land are filled
with produce.

Castagne, or chestnuts, in ancient times were essential for survival in the mountainous regions of Campania. Chestnuts are typically harvested from October through December. Dried in barns or attics, and then exposed to smoke and heat, chestnuts are versatile ingredients that can be made into flour or jam, and eaten fresh or dried.

The chestnuts from Avellino are heralded for their starchy density, pure white color, and sweetness. Traditionally these prized chestnuts are incorporated into the cuisine by serving them with wild boar or as a chestnut flour cake. But the most famous chestnuts are grown in Salerno, specifically Cilento. They boast a PGI (protected geographical indication) mark, which traces chestnuts back to their geographical origin for at least one phase of production. Chestnuts are ubiquitous in Sorrento, served often at home and also at restaurants. Viewed as a regional symbol of autumn, the nuts' delicate flavor is well paired with heftier dishes, such as a pureed pumpkin and chestnut soup or chestnut and legume soup; or paired with porcini mushrooms and homemade pasta.

Roasted chestnuts are a holiday favorite and can be candied and glazed—*marrons glacés*, a French specialty that dates back to the sixteenth century—or baked into traditional Christmas cookies. While the flavor and fragrance of chestnuts is unparalleled, peeling chestnuts is labor-intensive work.

In the fall, the mountain villages of the Amalfi Coast are filled with prickly chestnuts. Each year, the town of Scala celebrates the nut at the Festa della castagna, or Chestnut Festival.

ZUPPA DI CASTAGNE
E LEGUMI

Chestnut and legume soup

— ½ cup (100 g) pearl barley
— ½ cup (100 g) lentils
— ½ cup (100 g) dried peas
— ½ cup (100 g) dried cannellini
   beans
— ½ cup (100 g) dried chickpeas
— about ½ cup (100 ml)
   olive oil
— 1 onion, thinly sliced
— 1 carrot, finely chopped
— 1 stalk celery, finely chopped
— 1 tomato, diced
— 1 clove garlic, peeled
   but whole
— 4 sage leaves
— 1 sprig rosemary
— 14 oz (400 g) fresh chestnuts,
   shelled and peeled
— salt and pepper

For serving
— 6–8 slices bread, toasted
— olive oil, for drizzling
— chopped chili pepper
   (optional)

Typical of the Cilento countryside, this soup is also known as *cicci marretati*. It was often served as a main course thanks to its high calorie content.

Preparation time: 40 minutes + 12 hours soaking
Cooking time: about 2 hours
Serves 6–8

In separate bowls, cover the barley, lentils, peas, beans, and chickpeas with water and soak for 12 hours. Drain and set aside.

Heat the oil in a large pan. Add the onion, carrot, celery, tomato, and garlic and stir until soft. Remove the garlic as soon as it browns. Add the soaked legumes, enough cold water to cover the vegetables and legumes, the sage and rosemary. Cover and cook for 45 minutes.

Add the chestnuts and cook, stirring from time to time, until everything is tender, about 45 minutes, adding hot water if necessary. Season with salt and pepper. Remove from the heat.

To serve: Place a piece of toast at the bottom of each bowl and ladle in the soup. Drizzle with olive oil, sprinkle with chili pepper (if using), and serve.

CUPOLA DI SPAGHETTI

Preparation time: 40 minutes
Cooking time: 45 minutes
Serves 8

Preheat the oven to 375°F (190°C/Gas Mark 5). Line a baking sheet with foil and butter a springform pan.

Cook the spaghetti in a large pot of boiling water halfway to al dente.

Meanwhile, in separate pans of boiling water, cook the beans and carrots until crisp-tender. Drain and toss each with 1 tablespoon of the butter, and season with salt and pepper. Transfer to a bowl.

Melt 1 tablespoon of the butter in a small frying pan and gently sauté the zucchini until tender. Season with salt and pepper. Add the zucchini to the green beans and carrots.

When the pasta is half cooked, drain and toss with the remaining 4 tablespoons butter, the Parmesan and grated caciocavallo. Measure out two-thirds of the spaghetti mixture for lining the springform pan and set aside. Add the eggs and the vegetables to the remaining spaghetti and set aside.

To make the dome, line the prepared springform pan with the reserved spaghetti-cheese mixture, starting from the middle to create a spiral. Fill the dome with the spaghetti and vegetable mixture, cover with foil, place on the lined baking sheet and bake for 20 minutes.

Take the dome out of the oven, let stand for 5 minutes, then turn the dome out onto an ovenproof serving dish. Cover the surface with the slices of provolone and return to the oven until the cheese has completely melted. Take out of the oven and garnish with the reserved beans and carrots.

Spaghetti dome

— 7 tablespoons (3½ oz/100 g) butter
— 12 oz (350 g) spaghetti
— ¼ lb (100 g) green beans, cut into 1-inch (2.5 cm) lengths
— 2 medium ¼ lb (100 g) carrots, chopped
— salt and pepper
— 1 small (100 g) zucchini (courgette), chopped
— 1½ oz (40 g) Parmesan cheese, grated
— 2 tablespoons grated caciocavallo or provolone cheese
— 2 eggs, lightly beaten
— ¼ lb (100 g) mild provolone cheese, thinly sliced

CACIOCAVALLO CHEESE

Caciocavallo is a pale yellow cow's milk cheese hailing from the Apennine mountains of Campania, and traditionally made in the region of Avellino. Eaten fresh, aged, or smoked, this ancient variety of cheese is thought to have been produced in Italy since the fourteenth century. Directly translated as "horse cheese," caciocavallo is matured by hanging pairs of gourd-shaped cheeses from a horizontal pole, giving the illusion that the cheese is hanging over a saddle. Caciocavallo may come from the Latin word *cascabellus*, meaning sleigh bell or rattle.

A member of the *pasta filata* family—"spun paste," which refers to cheese made by stretching the curds —caciocavallo has a soft, springy texture, enclosed in a tough, edible rind. Warm curds are stretched into the shape of a ball, which is then sealed in shape by plunging the ball into boiling water. Cooled in cold water, the cheese is then cured in brine and hung over poles. It must be aged for two weeks at minimum and continually exposed to humidity in caves. The longer the cheese ages, the saltier, sharper, and more complex the flavor becomes.

Several varieties of caciocavallo exist, differentiated by the breed of cow (such as the Podolico or Godrano) whose milk is used to make the cheese.

Page 162:
Sea kayaks are an exciting way to explore the coast's many grottos.

Page 163:
The Lattari Mountains wind their way between the gulfs of Naples and Salerno, diving into the Mediterranean Sea.

The texture and flavor of caciocavallo make it a perfect stand-in for aged provolone or even Parmesan.

MELANZANE ALLA PARMIGIANA

Preparation time: 1 hour 35 minutes
Cooking time: 1 hour 30 minutes
Serves 6

Cut the eggplants vertically into slabs ¼ inch (0.5 cm) thick. Arrange the slices in a bowl and sprinkle with salt. Press down with a weight and let sit for 1 hour.

In the meantime, to make the tomato sauce: Bring a small pan of water to a boil. With a paring knife, make an "X" through the skin on the bottom of each tomato (do not slice into the flesh). Plunge the tomatoes into the boiling water until the skin at the "X" begins to peel away from the flesh, 1–2 minutes (depending on how ripe the tomatoes are). Run under cold water. Once cool, peel the tomatoes, remove the seeds and cores, and chop. Drain in a fine-mesh sieve. Discard any juices. Combine the tomatoes, a few basil leaves, and a pinch of salt and pepper in a shallow pan. Cook over high heat for 20 minutes and then pass the sauce through a food mill.

Preheat the oven to 350°F (180°C/Gas Mark 4).

Rinse and dry the eggplants thoroughly. Heat the oil in a frying pan. Fry the eggplants in batches until golden brown. Remove the eggplants and drain them thoroughly on a plate lined with paper towels.

Spread a few tablespoons of tomato sauce on the bottom of a 12 ½ x 10 inch (32 x 26 cm) baking dish, arrange a layer of eggplant slices, sprinkle with a little Parmesan, cover with a few slices of mozzarella, scatter a few basil leaves, and finish with 3–4 tablespoons of beaten egg. Continue layering until the ingredients are used up, ending with slices of eggplant, tomato sauce, and knobs of butter. Bake for 30 minutes. Serve.

Eggplant Parmesan

— 4–5 eggplants (aubergines)
— salt
— 1 lb 2 oz (500 g) San Marzano tomatoes
— basil leaves
— pepper
— 2 cups (500 ml) olive oil
— ⅔ cup (60 g) grated Parmesan cheese
— 3½ oz (100 g) mozzarella cheese, sliced
— 2 eggs, beaten
— 1½ tablespoons (20 g) butter

CANNELLONI ALLA SORRENTINA

Sorrento-style cannelloni

— 6 vertical slices (¼ inch/
    0.5 cm thick) eggplant
    (aubergine)
— salt
— 9 oz (250 g) fior di latte
    mozzarella cheese
— 2 red bell peppers
— 12 squares (3–4 inch/8–
    10 cm) egg pasta (from
    Ravioli Capresi, page 60)
— oil for drizzling
— 1 tablespoon (½ oz/10 g)
    butter
— basil leaves
— black pepper
— scant ½ cup (50 g) grated
    Parmesan or pecorino cheese
— scant 1 cup (200 ml) tomato
    purée (passata)

Preparation time: 2 hours
Cooking time: 1 hour 20 minutes
Serves 6

Arrange the eggplant slices in a bowl and sprinkle with salt. Press down with a weight and let sit for 1 hour.

Cut the fior di latte into strips and drain in a sieve.

Preheat the oven to 400°F (200°C/Gas Mark 6).

Roast the peppers for 30 minutes, turning them over after 15 minutes. Remove from the oven but leave the oven on and reduce the temperature to 350°F (180°C/Gas Mark 4). When the peppers are cool enough to handle, peel and seed them. Cut into strips and let drain on paper towels.

Meanwhile, make the pasta as directed and cut into squares. Cook the pasta squares in a large pot of salted boiling water until al dente. Plunge in cold water, drain, and allow to rest for 15 minutes.

Rinse and dry the eggplant thoroughly. Drizzle some oil on the bottom of a shallow baking dish and arrange the eggplant in the dish. Drizzle with more oil. Bake until browned on both sides. Remove from the oven but leave the oven on.

Butter a baking dish that will hold the 12 cannelloni snugly. Divide the eggplant, bell pepper, mozzarella, and basil among the 12 pasta squares. Season with salt and black pepper. Sprinkle with the Parmesan or pecorino. Roll up the pasta squares, arrange them in the baking dish, and cover with the tomato purée and knobs of butter. Bake for 20 minutes. Remove from the oven and let stand for 5–10 minutes before serving.

SQUID

Page 174:
Many beaches are
accessed by long flights
of stairs carved into the
rocky coast.

Page 175:
Bathers take a break from
the hot summer sun.

Campania is well regarded for its plethora of seafood,
especially in regions with close proximity to the
sea, such as Sorrento or the Amalfi Coast. Many harbor
towns are famous for their fishing and have a long
history of ancient techniques still employed today.
Among other fish, the locals fish for squid, a member
of the cephalopod family with a bilateral body, tentacles,
and an obtrusive head. Similar to octopus or cuttlefish,
squid have ink sacs they use to deter predators.

When cooking squid, the head and innards are
discarded. The body and tentacles (which are edible)
are rinsed clean. The body is then ready for slicing
or leaving whole for stuffing.

Best paired with lemon and herbs, Campania boasts
several famous squid dishes such as *totani alla sorrentina*
(page 178), squid stuffed with mozzarella and
caciocavallo and simmered in a simple tomato sauce.
Pasta con i calamari is pasta with squid in tomato
and wine sauce. *Risotto alla pescatora*, fisherman's rice,
is prepared with clams, squid, mussels, and shrimp
(prawns), and enriched by a broth simmered with
the shells.

The most popular squid dishes include fried calamari,
in which squid is thinly sliced, and the rings and
tentacles are briefly dipped in batter, fried, and served
with lemon. The Neapolitan seafood salad, *insalata di
mare*—consisting of squid, shrimp (prawns), octopus,
lemon, and parsley—is often served on Christmas Eve
as part of the Feast of the Seven Fishes, or The Vigil,
a southern Italian tradition. Fried calamari is often
included.

Squid is a common
ingredient in the seafood-
rich rice dish, *risotto alla
pescatora.*

Sorrento-style squid

— 20 San Marzano or plum
   tomatoes
— 2 eggs
— 11 oz (300 g) mozzarella
   cheese, chopped
— 1 oz (30 g) caciocavallo or
   Parmesan cheese, grated
— 8 tablespoons breadcrumbs
— 1¼ teaspoon crushed chili
   pepper flakes
— salt and black pepper
— 4 lb (1.8 kg) squid, cleaned
— ½ cup (100 ml) olive oil
— 1 clove garlic, peeled
   but whole
— 2 tablespoons chopped
   parsley

Preparation time: 40 minutes
Cooking time: 1 hour 10 minutes
Serves 6

Bring a small pan of water to a boil. With a paring knife, make an "X" through the skin on the bottom of each tomato (do not slice into the flesh). Plunge the tomatoes into the boiling water until the skin at the "X" begins to peel away from the flesh, 1– 2 minutes (depending on how ripe the tomatoes are). Run under cold water. Once cool, peel the tomatoes, remove the seeds and cores, and chop. Drain in a fine-mesh sieve. Discard any juices.

To make the filling, mix together the eggs, mozzarella, caciocavallo, breadcrumbs, chili flakes, and a pinch of salt and black pepper.

Stuff each squid with the prepared mixture and fold the tentacles inward to close them securely.

Heat the oil in a pan and brown the garlic. Remove and discard the garlic. Add the parsley and tomatoes and season with salt. Cook for 5 minutes. Add the squid, season with salt and black pepper, cover, and cook over low heat for about 1 hour. Serve the squid whole or sliced.

TIELLA ALLA CILENTANA

Preparation time: 45 minutes
Cooking time: 35–40 minutes
Serves 6–8

To prepare the seafood broth, combine the shrimp shells and water in a pot. Bring to a boil and simmer for 45 minutes. Strain and reserve.

In a small bowl, dissolve the saffron in a spoonful of hot water and a spoonful of hot seafood broth.

Preheat the oven to 400°F (200°C/Gas Mark 6).

Heat the oil in a Dutch oven (casserole). Add the onion and celery and sauté for 5 minutes. Add the monkfish and the shrimp and cook for a few minutes. Add the bell pepper, peas, and tomatoes and season with salt. Add the wine and continue cooking for 10 minutes. Add the rice and saffron mixture. Cover the dish and bring to a boil. Transfer the dish to the oven and bake for 18 minutes. Remove from the oven, add the butter, and shake the dish slightly. Sprinkle with parsley and serve immediately.

Cilento-style casserole

— 1 lb (500 g) shrimp (prawns), peeled and shells reserved
— scant 1 cup (200 ml) water
— pinch of saffron
— ½ cup (100 ml) olive oil
— 1 white onion, thinly sliced
— 1 stalk celery, chopped
— 2¼ lb (1 kg) monkfish, cut into small pieces
— 1 yellow bell pepper, sliced
— scant 2 cups (250 g) peas
— 9 oz (250 g) canned whole tomatoes
— salt
— ½ cup (100 ml) dry white wine
— 1¼ cups (250 g) carnaroli or Arborio rice
— 2 tablespoons (1 oz/30 g) butter
— 2 tablespoons chopped parsley

INSALATA DI LIMONI DI SORRENTO

Preparation time: 20 minutes + 12 hours marinating
Serves 4

Add the lemon slices to a bowl and cover with cold water. Add the salt, chili pepper, and vinegar. Cover and let marinate for 12 hours, or until the pith has softened.

Drain the lemon slices, place them in a bowl, and drizzle with the olive oil. Season with more salt and vinegar, if necessary. Serve sprinkled with parsley.

Sorrento lemon salad

— 3 lemons, washed, thinly sliced, and seeded
— 1 teaspoon coarse salt
— 1 large fresh red chili pepper, sliced into thin rings
— 2 tablespoons distilled white vinegar
— 4–5 tablespoons olive oil
— 2 tablespoons chopped parsley

LEMONS

The intensely flavored and succulent lemons of
Sorrento and the Amalfi Coast are a celebrated culinary
symbol of Campania. The fruit thrives in the fertile
soil and has a lengthy and important history in
international trade and regional production. Lemons
are ubiquitous throughout Campania and have been
so since Roman times. They are even depicted on
ceramics and on the frescoes of Pompeii.

The *limone Costa d'Amalfi* is grown on the Amalfi
Coast and is also called *sfusato amalfitano*. This variety
is as fragrant as the Sorrento version, but has knobby
ends, fewer seeds, and more vitamin C. The lemons are
typically washed and peeled by hand within two days
of harvesting to protect their aroma.

Sorrento boasts *limone di Sorrento* or *ovale di Sorrento*,
which are larger, oval-shaped, and juicier than the
Amalfi lemons, and can be eaten raw. In addition to
being intensely fragrant, both are honored by their
PGI (protected geographical indication) status, which
specifies that the lemons were grown in the Amalfi
or Sorrento areas and were ripened according to
traditional regulations.

Sorrento lemons are grown under *pagliarelle*, straw
mats, which cover the tops of the lemon trees. The
purpose of the *pagliarelle* is to delay ripening. Hilly
terraced gardens, which slope toward the ocean, are
usually lined with wooden stakes. The wood supports
the *pagliarelle*, in addition to creating picturesque
pergolas. Lemon pergolas have become a conspicuous
and seductive part of the Sorrento landscape.

Both versions of lemons are used for limoncello,
the lemon-flavored liqueur, by soaking the peels and
releasing the essential oils into alcohol, which is
then mixed with a simple syrup. Limoncello is often
served as an after-dinner digestive. The zest of

Pages 182—183:
Many of the shop exteriors
in Vietri sul Mare are
covered in ceramic tiles.
The ceramics there are all
painted by hand.

Lemons were first
brought to the Amalfi
Coast centuries ago on
trade routes from the
Middle East.

Campania lemons can be used in *struffoli* (page 216), a traditional Neapolitan Christmas dish, as well as in cooling and refreshing granitas, which remain popular throughout Campania. Lemons are often candied for use in various desserts, such as the *pastiera napoletana* (page 101), an Easter wheat and ricotta pie. Lemons possess a more savory purpose as well, as seen in the *insalata di limoni di Sorrento* (page 185), Sorrento lemon salad.

Roadside shops sell lemon-based products such as limoncello, *crema di limoncello*, and lemon baba.

PIZZA MARGHERITA

Preparation time: 20 minutes + 35 minutes rising
Cooking time: 20 minutes
Makes 2 small pizzas or 1 large pizza

Make the pizza dough, roll out, and line the pan(s) as directed in the dough recipe. Cover with a kitchen towel and let rest for 20 minutes.

Preheat the oven to 475°F (250°C/Gas Mark 9).

Meanwhile, to make the topping: Bring a small pan of water to a boil. With a paring knife, make an "X" through the skin on the bottom of each tomato (do not slice into the flesh). Plunge the tomatoes into the boiling water until the skin at the "X" begins to peel away from the flesh, 1–2 minutes (depending on how ripe the tomatoes are). Run under cold water. Once cool, peel the tomatoes, remove the seeds and cores, and chop. Drain in a fine-mesh sieve. Discard any juices.

When the dough is ready, evenly spread the chopped tomatoes over the top(s) of the pizza(s) leaving a ½-inch (1 cm) border all around. Add the salt, drizzle generously with oil, and bake for 10 minutes. Remove from the oven and cover the surface with the mozzarella and a few basil leaves. Return to the oven and bake until the outer crust is thoroughly browned, 10–12 minutes. Serve hot.

Margherita pizza

— Pizza Dough (page 265)

For the topping
— 8 San Marzano or plum tomatoes
— pinch of salt
— olive oil, for drizzling
— 9–11 oz (250–300 g) mozzarella cheese, thinly sliced and drained
— basil leaves

SAN MARZANO TOMATOES

The most praised tomatoes of Italy, with a memorable, peculiar shape and a bright red color, San Marzano tomatoes are famous for many reasons. Grown in rich, fertile, volcanic soil, they are often referred to as Mt. Vesuvius tomatoes. The tomatoes boast a supreme sweetness, low acidity, and firm flesh. With only two seed pockets (other varieties often have at least four) and a thin skin, these vibrant heirloom plants are a variety of plum tomatoes. Well suited for cooking, they are considered the only tomatoes fit for a true Neapolitan pizza sauce.

Tomatoes have been grown in Italy since the Middle Ages, but originated in Peru and Mexico. Introduced by the Spanish, tomatoes were mostly grown for ornamental purposes. Cloaked in superstition, tomatoes were seen as mysterious, maybe poisonous, and used as a stimulant or aphrodisiac. They were finally discovered as edible in the nineteenth century.

The harvest is short and runs from August through September. Because of their delicate nature, these tomatoes must be gently picked by hand when they are exactly ripe. San Marzano tomatoes hold an official DOP (protected designation of origin) label, and multiple, strict regulations exist for growing. As a result of the expensive labor required to harvest these extraordinary tomatoes, production costs are high.

Though most of the world only knows canned San Marzano tomatoes, they are a common sight in local markets.

PIZZA CON INSALATA DI POMODORI

Preparation time: 35 minutes + 20 minutes rising
Cooking time: 30 minutes
Makes 1 large pizza

Make the pizza dough as directed in the dough recipe.
Oil a 12½ x 18-inch (25 x 45 cm) rimmed baking
sheet. Roll out the dough and fit it into the pan.
Cover with a kitchen towel and let rest for 20 minutes.

To make the topping: Add the tomatoes to a large
bowl and add the basil, oregano, garlic, salt, and
3 tablespoons of the oil. Toss to combine and marinate
for at least 30 minutes.

Meanwhile, preheat the oven to 450°F (230°C/Gas
Mark 8).

Drain the tomato salad and spread over the dough.
Drizzle with the remaining 1 tablespoon olive oil.
Bake until the dough is golden brown, 25 – 30 minutes.

Pizza with tomato salad

— Pizza Dough Base (page 265)

For the topping
— 10 San Marzano or plum
   tomatoes, cut into ½-inch
   (1 cm) pieces
— ¼ cup basil, chopped
— 2 tablespoons minced
   fresh oregano
— 2 cloves garlic, minced
— 1 teaspoon salt
— 4 tablespoons olive oil

PIZZA DI BACCALÀ

Salt cod pizza

— 1 lb 2 oz (500 g) salt cod

For the dough
— 1 envelope (¼ oz/7 g)
   active dry yeast
— ¼ cup (50 g) granulated sugar
— warm water
— salt
— 3¾ cups (400 g) 00 flour
— 9 tablespoons (4½ oz/125 g)
   lard or butter, at room
   temperature

For the filling
— 4 tablespoons olive oil
— 1 clove garlic, minced
— 1¾ lb (800 g) escarole,
   rinsed, trimmed, and sliced
   into ½-inch (1 cm) ribbons
— 3 oz (70 g) pitted black olives
— 2 tablespoons capers, rinsed
— 3 oz (80 g) anchovy fillets,
   chopped
— 2 tablespoons chopped
   parsley

Preparation time: 1 hour + 2 hours 15 minutes
rising + 24 hours soaking
Cooking time: 1 hour
Serves 10–12

Soak the salt cod in a bowl of water in the refrigerator
for 24 hours, periodically changing the water. Drain well.

Stir together the yeast and a pinch of the sugar in a
little warm water. Set aside for 10–15 minutes. Dissolve
a pinch of salt in a glass of warm water.

In a stand mixer, combine the flour, yeast mixture, lard,
and remaining sugar. Gradually add the salted water
to make a cohesive dough and knead for 5 minutes.
Cover and let rise at room temperature for 2 hours.

Preheat the oven to 375°F (190°C/Gas Mark 5).
Grease and flour a 10½-inch (26 cm) cake pan.

To make the filling: Heat 3 tablespoons of the oil
in a large frying pan over medium-high heat. Add the
garlic, escarole, ½ cup (100 ml) water, and half the
olives and capers. Cook until the liquid has evaporated.
Add half the anchovies and remove from the heat.

Meanwhile, heat the remaining 1 tablespoon oil in
a frying pan and sauté the salt cod with the remaining
capers, olives, and anchovies for 10 minutes. Cook
until the fish is flaky and opaque. Stir in the parsley
and remove from the heat to cool.

Punch the dough down, divide in half, and roll to
10½-inch (27 cm) rounds. Fit one round into the cake
pan. Layer in half the escarole mixture, cover with the
salt cod, and top with the remaining escarole. Cover
with the second round of dough, tucking the edges
under to seal. Bake until a deep, golden brown, about
40 minutes. Serve hot or warm.

ANCHOVIES

Anchovies are a familiar ingredient throughout the Campania region. These miniature, preserved fish typically add a subtle, umami flavor, but can also lend a more pronounced bite to many regional dishes. The savory flavor of anchovies is showcased in *gonfietti* (page 38), an addictive snack made of fried anchovy-seasoned dough.

The majority of anchovy fishing occurs on the Amalfi Coast, where fishermen follow the ancient practice of capturing anchovies in nets. The best quality anchovies have their heads immediately removed after being caught. The anchovies are then rinsed in brine to remove the blood, thus creating firmer fish for the preservation process.

Menaica anchovies are a specialty product that comes typically from the Cilento Coast, nearby Salerno. During the spring and summer, in a process known as *menaica*, the local fishermen use special nets and fish by moonlight, which attracts the anchovies. Jars of *menaica* anchovies are known by their pale, pink flesh.

As soon as anchovies are caught, they are cleaned and coated in sea salt. The salted fish is layered in a small wooden barrel, sealed, and weighted. This liquid that rises to the top is captured and stored in cool rooms for further aging. The result of this is *colatura di alici*. Essentially an Italian fish sauce, the clear, amber-colored condiment has a full and intense flavor. It's used to add flavor to vegetables, such as escarole or potatoes, and can be simply tossed with spaghetti, lemon zest, garlic, and parsley.

Another way of preserving anchovies is to tightly pack the deboned fish in olive oil or vinegar. These anchovies are often ground up with oil and salt and sold in tubes as anchovy paste.

Page 198:
Houses are built into the rock, nearly blending in with their surroundings.

Page 199:
Passageways offer much-needed shade during the summer months.

The small fishermen's village of Cetara has a long tradition of both anchovy and tuna fishing. The town is famous for its local production of the Italian fish sauce called *colatura di alici*.

PIZZA ALLA CAMPOFRANCO

Preparation time: 30 minutes + 1 hour 30 minutes rising
Cooking time: 45 minutes
Serves 6–8

To make the dough: Dissolve the yeast and sugar in a little warm water. Let rest for 10–15 minutes.

In the bowl of a stand mixer fitted with a dough hook, combine the flour and salt and pepper to taste. Add the lard, 4 beaten eggs, and finally the yeast mixture. Knead the dough vigorously, adding a little warm water if necessary to make a cohesive dough, about 5 minutes. Cover and let rise in a warm place for 30 minutes.

Preheat the oven to 375°F (190°C/Gas Mark 5). Grease and flour a 9-inch (24 cm) round cake pan.

To make the filling: Heat the oil in a frying pan over medium heat. Once the oil is hot, add the tomatoes and salt and cook until most of the moisture has evaporated, 8–10 minutes. Set aside.

Punch the dough down and divide into two slightly uneven parts. Roll the smaller ball out to 9 inches (24 cm) and the larger ball out to 12 inches (30 cm). Line the prepared pan with the 12-inch (30 cm) round, allowing it to come up the sides. Fill the dough-lined pan with half the mozzarella and then alternating layers of the Parmesan, tomatoes, prosciutto, and basil. Top with the remaining mozzarella. Cover with the smaller 9-inch (24 cm) dough round. Tuck in any edges and seal the dough together. Set aside to rise for 1 hour.

Brush the dough with the remaining beaten egg and bake until the dough is golden brown and cooked through, about 45 minutes. Serve the pizza warm or at room temperature.

Campofranco-style pizza

For the dough
— 2 envelopes (¼ oz/7 g each) active dry yeast
— ½ teaspoon granulated sugar
— warm water, as needed
— 3 cups (400 g) all-purpose (plain) flour
— salt and pepper
— 10 tablespoons (5 oz/150 g) lard or butter, at room temperature
— 5 eggs

For the filling
— 2 tablespoons olive oil
— 2 lb 4 oz (1 kg) canned San Marzano tomatoes, drained and chopped
— pinch of salt
— 14 oz (400 g) mozzarella cheese, thinly sliced
— ¾ cups (80 g) grated Parmesan cheese
— 7 oz (200 g) prosciutto, thinly sliced
— ½ cup chopped basil

CACIORICOTTA CHEESE

A young, full-fat springtime goat cheese, typically produced in Cilento in the region of Salerno, *cacioricotta* has a tangy and mildly spicy flavor. Cilento is well known for its goats, specifically the Cilentana herd. They enjoy grazing on Cilento terrain and the flavor of the cheese reflects the unique topography of Cilento.

However, *cacioricotta* can also be made with cow's or sheep's milk, in addition to goat's milk. Similar to ricotta salata, and used in the same ways, the semisoft cheese is formed into a compact, cylindrical shape. The cheese can be eaten fresh for a sweeter flavor, or aged three to four months for a more intense, salty seasoning. The color changes from alabaster to a more golden hue as the cheese ages.

This traditional cheese can be produced according to artisanal or industrial methods. Similar to ricotta, rennet is added to the milk as it is brought to a boiling point, and then the milk mixture is rapidly cooled.

The solid cheese is best served with wine, olives, and taralli (page 115), a savory fennel cracker unique to Campania.

Cacioricotta is traditionally grated over pasta.

CASATIELLO RUSTICO

This country-style tart known as *casatiello* is eaten at Easter. Full of flavor, the golden brown ring represents the Resurrection and the arrival of spring.

Preparation time: 30 minutes + about 5 hours rising
Cooking time: 1 hour
Serves 10–12

Dissolve the yeast in a little warm water and set aside for 10–15 minutes.

Pile the flour on a work surface and make a well in the center. Add 4 tablespoons of the lard, the yeast mixture, a pinch of salt and enough warm water to obtain a fairly soft dough. Knead vigorously for about 10 minutes. Form a ball, cover, and let rise in a warm place until doubled in volume, about 2 hours.

Punch the dough down and flatten to a rectangle ½ inch (1 cm) thick. Spread with 2 tablespoons of lard. Sprinkle with pepper to taste and 1 tablespoon Parmesan. Fold the dough in half, brush with 1 tablespoon lard, sprinkle with the remaining 1 tablespoon Parmesan, and add the salami, pecorino, and pepper to taste. Fold the dough in half, flatten to a rectangle ½ inch (1 cm) thick, and spread it with another tablespoon of lard. Repeat this last step until there is only 1 tablespoon of lard left. Pull off a piece of dough the size of a bread roll, spread it with the remaining tablespoon of lard, and leave to rise for 3 hours. Brush a 12 inch (30 cm) shallow tube pan with oil. Roll the remaining dough into a thick log and fit it in the mold. Cover and let rise for 3 hours.

Preheat the oven to 350°F (180°C/Gas Mark 4). Place the eggs over the dough. Roll the reserved dough into a rope ⅛ inch (3 mm) thick and cut crosswise into 12 strips. Cross two strips over each egg. Bake until golden brown, about 1 hour. Let cool before serving.

Rustic Easter bread

— 2 envelopes (¼ oz/7 g each) active dry yeast
— warm water
— 4½ cups (600 g) all-purpose (plain) flour
— 16 tablespoons (8 oz/225 g) lard or butter, at room temperature
— salt and pepper
— 2 tablespoons grated Parmesan cheese
— 7 oz (200 g) Neapolitan salami (or any spicy, smoky salami), diced
— 1 tablespoon grated Pecorino Romano cheese
— olive oil, for the pan
— 6 eggs

LIMONCELLO

Limoncello, a strong lemon liqueur unique to Campania, is made with the zest (the thin colored layer of the peels) of either Sorrento or Amalfi lemons, considered to be the only varieties worth using. Most important, the lemons should be as fresh as possible, even if they are green and not yet the trademark sunny yellow.

The lemon zest is combined with a neutral spirit and sugar syrup and left to sit for about one month. Limoncello is so revered in the region that many families and restaurants have their own unique versions and recipes. However, the liqueur is also commercially produced and widely available. The drink is often packaged in decorative bottles and is a popular tourist souvenir or gift.

Many legends blur limoncello's origins and several areas within and outside Campania claim parentage. Popular lore is that the liqueur became known through Signora Vicenza Canale, the owner of a historic *pensione* "Mariantonia." At the end of meals, she would offer her guests a digestive of homemade limoncello. Her guests would sip it quietly as the sun set on Capri over the Gulf of Naples. However, Sorrento and the Amalfi Coast also claim responsibility for limoncello, as does the region of Liguria.

Limoncello is lighter than the majority of digestives, and is served ice cold in small, chilled glasses, or in a decorative ceramic glass. To reach maximum coldness, limoncello can also be stored in the freezer—and because of its high alcohol content it won't freeze. The digestive can also serve as the base for a Champagne cocktail, or diluted with tonic water or seltzer. Limoncello granita is a decadent and refreshing dessert as are limoncello cookies.

Several varieties of limoncello exist, including *crema di limoncello*, a creamy version made with cream and milk.

Pages 210–211: A home near Ravello in the interior's lush Lattari Mountains.

SFOGLIATELLE FROLLE

There are two varieties of *sfogliatella*: *riccia*, made with crisp, layered puff pastry, and *frolla*, a more accessible short dough, which tastes similar to a shortbread or pie crust. *Sfogliatella* is often served with coffee and is a favorite of Neapolitans.

Preparation time: 1 hour
Cooking time: 25–30 minutes
Makes 12

To make the dough: Combine the flour, sugar, salt, and lard in a food processor. Pulse until the lard is the size of peas. Pulse in the yolks, one at a time, until combined. Add in 1 tablespoon of water at a time, pulsing, until the dough comes together in a ball. Let it rest at room temperature for 30 minutes.

Preheat the oven to 375°F (190°C/Gas Mark 5). Line two baking sheets with parchment paper.

To make the filling: Combine the semolina, water, and salt in a pan and cook for 8 minutes. Remove from the heat and let cool, about 10 minutes.

Cream the ricotta and sugar in a bowl. Beat in the egg yolks, vanilla, cinnamon, candied fruit or zest, and orange blossom water. Mix in the cooked semolina.

Divide the dough into 12 balls. On a floured surface, roll the dough out to rounds ½ inch (1 cm) thick.

Place 2 tablespoons filling on half of each round. Brush the edges of the dough with the egg white and fold in half. Brush the surface of the cakes with the beaten egg and arrange them on the baking sheets. Bake until fully browned, 15–18 minutes.

Let the cakes cool slightly. Serve warm, sprinkled with powdered sugar.

Short pastry cakes

For the dough
— 3 cups (400 g) sifted all-purpose (plain) flour, sifted
— 5 tablespoons (60 g) granulated sugar
— pinch of salt
— 13 tablespoons (6½ oz/180 g) lard or butter, chilled and cubed
— 3 egg yolks
— 3 tablespoons water, plus more if needed

For the filling
— ⅓ cup (50 g) semolina
— 2 cups (500 ml) water
— pinch of salt
— ¾ cup plus 1 tablespoon (7 oz/200 g) sheep's milk ricotta cheese
— ¾ cups (150 g) granulated sugar
— 2 egg yolks
— 1 teaspoon vanilla extract
— ¼ teaspoon ground cinnamon
— 2 oz (60 g) candied orange peel, finely chopped, or 1 teaspoon grated orange zest
— 2 teaspoons orange blossom water (optional)

— 1 egg white
— 1 large egg, beaten
— Powdered (icing) sugar

SFOGLIATELLE

A *sfogliatella* is a shell-shaped pastry with a golden, layered crust, unique to Campania (the translation of *sfogliatella* is "thin leaf," or layer). The pastry is filled with the traditional mixture of ricotta, cooked semolina, sugar, and eggs. The rich and creamy mixture is flavored with orange zest or orange blossom water, marzipan, and candied citron. Sometimes a sprinkling of heady, warm cinnamon can be detected. The dough is stretched or rolled out by hand or by using a pasta roller, then brushed with lard or butter, which gives the pastry its unmistakable flaky layers. The dough is then rolled up into a cylindrical shape, which is sliced and individual rounds are rolled out, filled, and folded into a pocket, similar to the shape of a calzone. These treats are baked until golden brown and the layers of dough begin to separate.

Legend speculates that *sfogliatella* was originally prepared by a nun in the Conca dei Marini, Santa Rosa Monastery in Salerno in the seventeenth century. She created a sweet filling using cooked semolina, lemon liqueur, dried fruit, and sugar. She then enriched the dough with white wine and lard. The pastry was garnished with pastry cream and berries. However, a convent in Naples, Santa Croce di Lucca, also lays claim to the pastry.

Pasquale Pintauro, a Naples pastry chef, baked these treats in his shop to great acclaim in 1818. He eliminated the garnish of pastry cream and berries, and added ricotta cheese to the filling, and created a version called *riccia*, which uses a soft, flaky dough similar to puff pastry. A rounder shape of sfogliatella is frolla, which uses a short dough, however the filling is the same.

Page 218:
The region's extensive coastline and its easy access to fresh seafood has heavily influenced its cuisine.

Page 219:
Bougainvillea grows throughout the region, saturating the coast with its deep purple color.

Pages 222–223:
The Amalfi Coast is one of Italy's top spots for hiking. The region's trails were first carved in the Middle Ages to transport goods between villages.

STRUFFOLI

Struffoli are deep-fried balls of dough, often flavored with citrus or wine. Tossed in a honey glaze, they are then decorated, traditionally by children, with sugared almonds, sprinkles, cinnamon, candied pumpkin, or candied fruit. *Struffoli* range in size from marbles or hazelnuts to larger, gnocchi-like shapes. A holiday favorite, they are often used as a centerpiece for the table, piled vertically in a cone shape, or arranged in a circle and decorated like a wreath.

Originally descended from a Greek recipe, versions can also be found in Umbria and Calabria. The name likely comes from the Greek word *strongoulos*, meaning "rounded," but it is rumored that the name comes from the Italian verb *strofinare*, or rub; the action of kneading the egg and flour dough and then rolling it into a rope before cutting and shaping into round balls.

This festive dessert is a lengthy project best suited in the company of friends or family and many Italians consider *struffoli* a time-honored Christmas tradition.

STRUFFOLI

Struffoli

- 4 cups (500 g) all-purpose (plain) flour
- 1 teaspoon baking powder
- 4 tablespoons (2 oz/60 g) butter or lard, at room temperature
- 3 tablespoons granulated sugar
- pinch of salt
- grated zest of 4½ oranges
- 1 egg yolk
- 3 eggs
- ¼ cup (60 ml) dry white wine (optional)
- canola oil, for deep-frying
- 2 cups (1 lb 8 oz/700 g) honey
- candied orange and citron
- candied red cherries
- sprinkles

Preparation time: 40 minutes + 12 hours standing
Cooking time: 1 hour
Serves 4–6

Stir the flour and baking powder together in a bowl and form a well in the middle. Add the softened butter in pieces, 1½ tablespoons of the sugar, the salt, zest of ½ an orange, egg yolk, and whole eggs and mix together, adding wine if necessary to obtain a smooth mixture.

Divide the dough into 7 pieces and fold each piece of dough in half like a book, turn the folded piece of dough 90 degrees and fold again like a book. Without flouring the hands roll each piece of dough into a rope the thickness of a little finger, then cut crosswise into ½-inch (1 cm), yielding about 26 pieces per rope.

Pour enough oil into a medium Dutch oven (casserole) or heavy-bottomed pot to come halfway up the sides. Heat over medium-high heat until the oil reaches 350°F (180°C). Use a slotted spoon to drop in the *struffoli*, about 26 at a time. (Be careful as the oil will bubble up.) When the *struffoli* are golden brown, about 2 minutes, remove from the oil with the slotted spoon and drain on a plate lined with paper towels. Always bring the oil back to 350°F (180°C) before frying the next batch.

Combine the honey and remaining 1½ tablespoons sugar in a large pan over low heat and cook until the sugar is dissolved. Remove from the heat, add the *struffoli*, and mix until coated. Stir in the remaining orange zest. Carefully transfer the *struffoli* to a serving dish, form a dome shape and, with wet hands, carefully shape them (they may still be hot).

Decorate with candied fruit and sprinkles and let stand for at least 12 hours before serving.

MIGLIACCIO DOLCE

Semolina cake

— 2¾ cups (700 ml) water
— ¾ cup plus 2 tablespoons (150 g) semolina
— pinch of salt
— ½ cup (100 g) granulated sugar
— 1 teaspoon grated lemon zest
— 2 egg yolks
— 1 egg
— 1 teaspoon vanilla extract
— ⅔ cup (150 ml) milk, at room temperature
— Powdered (icing) sugar

The word *migliaccio* comes from the fact that the sweet was once made from millet (*miglio*) flour. It was later replaced with semolina and then yellow maize flour. If desired, raisins and pieces of candied orange and citron can also be added to the mixture.

Preparation time: 20 minutes
Cooking time: 1 hour 10 minutes
Serves 6–8

Preheat the oven to 350°F (180°C/Gas Mark 4). Grease and flour an 8-inch (20 cm) round cake pan.

Pour the water into a pan and bring to a boil. Stirring constantly, sprinkle in the semolina and salt. Cook for 8 minutes then remove from the heat. Transfer the semolina to a bowl to cool for about 10 minutes, stirring constantly.

Whisk in the sugar and lemon zest. Whisk in the egg yolks one at a time. Whisk in the whole egg, vanilla, and milk. It should be a fairly soft mixture at the end.

Pour the semolina mixture into the prepared pan and bake until the top of the cake is a dark, golden brown (the cake will have a runny, pudding-like texture), about 1 hour. Let cool. Serve sprinkled with powdered sugar.

IV

AVELLINO AND BENEVENTO

AVELLINO AND BENEVENTO

Hilly and located in a green valley, Benevento is a region of historical significance, Roman influence, and abundant folklore. In ancient times, Benevento served as a fortified military center for southern Italy, as the result of the meeting of several major roads, including the Via Appia, or Appian Way.

Benevento flourished during Roman times. Currently, tourists flock to the region to visit one of Campania's cultural treasures, the Arco di Traiano, Arch of Trajan, a preserved Roman arch erected in 114 AD with reliefs that depict Emperor Trajan's reign.

Benevento also served as the capital of the Lombards before they eventually moved east to Salerno in search of a harbor. A castle and set of ancient ruins still remain. The Duomo di Benevento was built in the seventh century, and in the thirteenth century, under papal rule, the church was transformed into a Romanesque cathedral. The area was heavily bombed during World War II, but has since been rebuilt. The cathedral's original, magnificent bronze doors still remain.

Cloaked in mystery and legend, Benevento has been called the "City of Witches." During Roman times, the Egyptian cult of Isis, a goddess of magic and mystery, found a hospitable home in Benevento. The vivid imagination of locals later encouraged the development of another cult, based on Wothan, father of gods, during the Lombards' rule. A sacred walnut tree, Noce di Benevento, encouraged open-air nature rituals and became a symbol of paganism, a belief that remained active despite the vast spread of Christianity throughout Italy. The tree was cut down in the seventh century. However, legend states that on certain evenings, witches can still be seen dancing on the tree's original site.

Page 224:
A doorway in the old town of Cusano Mutri.

The rustic mountain towns and green valleys of Avellino and Benevento contrast with the scenic coastline of the Amalfi Coast.

Benevento is well known for its wines, and boasts a high number of DOC vintages. The region tends to favor meat over fish, specifically pork, wild boar, and a variety of local cured meats. Benevento is famous for its regional specialty of *torrone*, an Italian nougat made with egg whites, honey, almonds or hazelnuts, and sometimes chocolate or citrus, as well as Strega, a liqueur containing a secret mixture of seventeen herbs and spices. Strega, whose name means witch, is often poured over fruit or ice cream.

The region of Avellino is situated northeast of Naples. In ancient times, Avellino was a geographically significant stopover on the road from Salerno to Benevento. Previously belonging to Benevento and Salerno, feudal rights were eventually acquired by an affluent Naples family who created the royal title Prince of Avellino. But peace was short lived, and in 1820, Avellino was the site of several riots. The region was bombed heavily in World War II and then disrupted by several earthquakes, most recently in 1980 and 1981. Located to the west, Mt. Vesuvius's continuous seismic activity has caused ash to fall upon Avellino. As a result, there has been an investment of funds to restore and improve infrastructure and promote economic expansion.

Located on a plain, surrounded by mountains, "Green Irpinia," as Avellino is often referred to, is a quiet area full of natural beauty. Rustic mountain towns, green valleys, waterfalls, and clear streams dominate the entrancing landscape, best explored by hiking or skiing. Lake Laceno, a mountain lake situated around woods, is a popular resort spot for holidays.

Agriculture is not a primary focus of the region, with the exception of tobacco and hazelnut crops. However, winemaking is so prevalent in this region, as a result of the fertile volcanic soil and ancient winemaking techniques, that the railway was once nicknamed Ferrovia del Vino, the wine train. Popular and awarded varieties of grapes include Fiano, Greco, and Aglianco. Traditional cheese making is also a specialty, as a result of two unique sheep breeds, resulting in specialized pecorino and ricotta cheeses.

Because of the distance from the sea, Avellino cuisine focuses primarily on pork and lamb, as well as cultivated and harvested mushrooms. Local black truffles adorn homemade pasta, and porcini are often served with tagliatelle. Sweet specialties include regional chestnut cakes and *spantorrone*, which is crumbly *torrone*, wrapped in sponge cake and then dipped in rum and Strega.

Pergolas are a common sight throughout the region.

Pages 232–233:
The ancient town of Cusano Mutri is nestled in the lush valley of Titerno.

SALSA DI FUNGHI
E PROSCIUTTO

*Mushroom and
prosciutto sauce*

— 1 oz (30 g) dried mushrooms
— 7 oz (200 g) prosciutto,
   finely chopped
— 2 tablespoons Marsala wine
— 7 tablespoons (3½ oz/100 g)
   butter
— ¾ cup (100 g) all-purpose
   flour
— 4¼ cups (1 liter) milk
— salt and pepper
— ⅔ cup (150 ml) heavy
   (double) cream

Preparation time: 30 minutes + 30 minutes soaking
Cooking time: 1 hour 15 minutes
Serves 8 – 10

Soak the mushrooms for 30 minutes in a pan of hot water. Place over medium heat and cook the mushrooms for 30 minutes. Drain through a sieve into a bowl. Finely chop the mushrooms.

Mix together the mushrooms, prosciutto, and the Marsala and set aside.

To make the béchamel: Heat butter in a medium saucepan over medium heat until melted. Whisk in the flour and cook for 2 minutes. Slowly pour in the milk, whisking the entire time, until combined. Bring the mixture to a boil, whisking the entire time, and simmer until thick enough to coat the back of a spoon, 3 – 5 minutes. Season with the salt and pepper.

Blend the béchamel, mushroom and ham mixture, and cream until smooth. Transfer to a medium saucepan and cook over low heat for 5 minutes.

Serve with roasts.

WINE

Italy is the largest producer of wine in the world, and Campania's terroir, Avellino's landscape in particular, has a history of producing some of the best wines. As a result of the mild climate—due to proximity to the Apennine mountain range; elevated topography; and mineral-rich, volcanic, fertile soil—Avellino is home to excellent and high-quality vineyards. Known for Taurasi, one of the region's best red wines, similar to a Brunello and Barolo; and Fiano, a dry and refreshing white wine. Both wines are awarded with DOCG (controlled and guaranteed designation of origin), which is the pinnacle of designation for Italian wines.

Taurasi wines are ubiquitous throughout the region. The wine is made from the Aglianico grape, widespread throughout southern Italy. As a result of the topography and soil, the grapes provide a strong, tannic bite, and thick, smoky taste; some say the wine tastes of chocolate. While not an ancient wine, the wine was awarded DOCG status in 1991. The wine must be composed of 85 percent Aglianico grapes and 15 percent local, red grapes; however most wines tend to be 100 percent Aglianico grapes. The wine must be aged a minimum of three years and stored in wood at least one year.

Fiano d'Avellino is created from the white Fiano grape, an ancient variety that dates back to cultivation by the Romans, and possibly even the Greeks. Often referred to as *vitis apiana*, or vine loved by bees, a name given by the Romans. This very sweet wine was greatly appreciated in the Middle Ages. The King of Naples was so enamored of the incredible sweetness of the wine, that he had vines planted in royal vineyards. Traditionally producing a low yield, in addition to secreting little juice, these grapes were considered to have low production value. However, the popularity of wine is such that producers now value quality over

The mild microclimate and mineral-rich, volcanic, and calcareous soils of the Apennine Mountains are a great benefit to the region's vineyards.

quantity as the wine is newly appreciated. Producers are encouraged to use the word *Apianum*, the ancient Roman wine, on the label to showcase the history of the ancient grape. Aficionados describe the wine as tasting delicately of quince, orange blossom, spice, and hazelnuts. The wine must be 85 percent Fiano grapes, and 15 percent Greco grapes or other local grapes. Perfect with pasta and clams, it is also ideal served alongside shellfish and other seafood.

Greco di Tufo, Campania's largest produced variety of white wine, is created from the Greco grapes, which are grown for both red (*nero*) or white (*bianco*) wines, in addition to creating a sparkling wine, *spumante*. The wine was transported to Campania by the Greeks more than 2,500 years ago. The term "Greco" can encompass a variety of wines, produced throughout Italy, but Greco di Tufo specifically comes from the vineyards of Avellino's town of Tufo and other neighboring villages. The word *tufo* derives from the word "tuff," a rock created by volcanic ash, which enhances the soil of Avellino, thus creating ideal growing conditions for vineyards. The wine must include 85 percent Greco grapes and is best served after a three- to four-year resting period.

The Fiano and Greco grapes were on the brink of extinction before being revived in the mid-twentieth century.

ZUPPA SANTÉ

This dish is traditionally served on Christmas day in the area of Solopaca. Some cookbooks call it *zuppa santé di nonna Carolina.*

Preparation time: 45 minutes
Cooking time: 1 hour
Serves 6

Mix the veal, egg, Parmesan, and a pinch of salt in a bowl. Take a little mixture at a time and form small balls.

Pour about 2 cups (500 ml) of the stock into a saucepan, bring to a boil, reduce the heat to a simmer. Add the meatballs and cook for a few minutes. Drain and set aside.

Bring the remaining 10 cups (2.5 liters) stock to a boil in a saucepan. Add the potatoes, celery, carrots, and onion and cook for 3–4 minutes. Add the escarole and cook for 3–4 minutes. Remove from the heat and set aside.

Divide the meatballs and mozzarella among 6 bowls. Ladle the vegetable stock over everything. Serve sprinkled with grated Parmesan.

Santé soup

— 1 lb 2 oz (500 g) ground (minced) veal
— 1 egg
— 2 tablespoons grated Parmesan cheese, plus more for serving
— salt
— 3 quarts (3 liters) capon or chicken stock
— ¾ lb (350 g) potatoes, peeled and cubed
— 4 stalks celery, diced
— 4 carrots, cubed
— 1 white onion, chopped
— 2 heads curly escarole, thinly shredded
— 11 oz (300 g) mozzarella cheese, cubed

TORTELLONI IN BRODO

Tortelloni in broth

— 30 squares (4 inch/10 cm)
    egg pasta (from Ravioli
    Capresi, page 60)
— 5 oz (150 g) cooked ham,
    finely chopped
— 1 large cooked chicken
    breast, finely chopped
— 1 cup (100 g) grated
    Parmesan cheese, plus
    more for serving
— salt and pepper
— scant 1 cup (200 ml)
    heavy (double) cream
— melted butter, for brushing
    the tortelloni
— 10 cups (2.5 liters)
    chicken stock

Preparation time: 1 hour
Cooking time: 40 minutes
Serves 3 – 5

Preheat the oven to 350°F (180°C/Gas Mark 4).
Grease a baking dish.

Cook the pasta in a large pot of boiling salted water
until al dente, then drain, rinse under cold water, and
spread out on a damp kitchen towel.

Place the ham and chicken in two separate bowls.
Dividing evenly, add the Parmesan. Season with salt
and pepper. Stir in enough cream to obtain a soft
mixture, but not too soft. Divide the chicken mixture
among 10 of the pasta squares and cover with the
same number of squares. Divide the ham mixture
among the 10 pasta packages, forming a second layer,
and cover with the remaining 10 pasta squares. Use
a round pasta cutter with a crimped edge to form
10 tortelloni. (These tortelloni can be made the day
before and kept in the fridge for up to 2 hours before
cooking. The traditional recipe also includes
mozzarella in the filling.)

Lay the tortelloni in the prepared baking dish, brush
each one with melted butter, cover the dish with foil,
and bake for 10 minutes. Remove the foil just before
the end of the cooking time to brown only slightly;
the tortelloni must remain soft.

When ready to serve, and while the tortelloni are
baking, bring the chicken stock to a boil.

Divide the tortelloni among shallow soup bowls and
ladle in the boiling stock. Serve with grated Parmesan
on the side.

LINGUINE AL PESTO
DI ZUCCHINE

Preparation time: 40 minutes
Cooking time: 40 minutes
Serves 6–8

Heat 3 tablespoons of oil in a small frying pan. Add the sliced almonds and cook, stirring from time to time, until browned. Set aside.

Bring a large pot of lightly salted water to a boil. Add the zucchini and cook until crisp-tender. Scoop out the zucchini and set aside to cool. Reserve the pot of cooking water.

In a blender or food processor, process the zucchini with the mint, parsley, chopped almonds, garlic, and Parmesan. With the machine running, drizzle in 10 tablespoons (150 ml) oil. Season with salt and pepper.

Bring the pot of reserved zucchini cooking water to a boil, add the pasta, and cook until al dente. Drain, transfer to a serving dish, and toss with the zucchini pesto. Drizzle with oil, season with pepper, and garnish with the toasted sliced almonds. Serve.

Linguine with zucchini pesto

— about ¾ cup (200 ml) olive oil
— 1½ oz (40 g) sliced almonds
— salt
— 1¼ lb (600 g) zucchini (courgette), halved lengthwise and seeded
— 25 mint leaves
— 2 tablespoons chopped parsley
— 2 oz (60 g) blanched almonds, chopped
— 1–2 cloves garlic, coarsely chopped
— 1⅓ cups (120 g) grated Parmesan cheese
— pepper
— 1¼ lb (600 g) linguine

ZUCCHINI

Developed in Italy, zucchini (courgette) is a squash that is harvested in the summer. Belonging to the same family as other squashes or pumpkins, zucchini is a fruit. Younger, smaller zucchini is desirable for its more nuanced flavor and tender flesh. When the zucchini is not yet mature, it can also include flowers, or blossoms, on the ends of the squash. Known as *fiori di zucca*, the flowers are edible, once the stamens or pistils are removed, and are considered a delicacy in Campania cuisine. The blossoms can be stuffed with a variety of cheeses, sometimes cured meats, battered, and fried. Male flowers, or flowers not attached to the zucchini, can be incorporated into a savory dough and fried in oil.

The bountiful zucchini harvest yields excellent dishes. Because of its delicate and clean flavor, zucchinis can be fried, preserved, grilled, marinated, stuffed, and briefly sautéed. A welcome accompaniment to pasta, zucchini is often served with clams. Instead of the traditional Italian red sauce, zucchini can be made into savory and luscious sauces for pasta, such as zucchini pesto (page 245).

Zucchine alle scapeche is a popular regional dish, based on a fish dish from Spain. A tart, vinegar-based marinade (*escabeche* in Spanish) is used to coat thin slices of zucchini instead of the traditional fish. The slices are then topped with mint and served as an antipasto. Another popular mainstay is *fritto misto*, in which zucchini slices are dipped in batter and briefly fried. Zucchini and artichokes are often soaked in flour and egg and deep-fried (*dorate e fritte*).

Zucchini (courgettes) will soak up oil and turn mushy instead of crisp if not salted and weighted properly to remove any excess moisture before cooking.

OLIVE OIL

Ravece olives grow throughout Irpinia. Their olive oil is excellent paired with seafood, grilled meats, or used to garnish salads and fresh cheeses.

Italy is the second largest producer of olive oil in Europe, second only to Spain, and is also the primary consumer: Olive oil is essential to Italian cuisine and dishes. Cilento, Salerno, and Sorrento all proudly produce olive oils with DOP (protected designation of origin) status. While it is unclear where olive trees originated, they are ubiquitous throughout the Mediterranean, and the oil was common to ancient Greeks and Romans for cosmetic and culinary use. Similar to a wine, olive oil can be judged and selected based on nuances of flavor, origin, and suitability to dishes.

Irpinia, in the region of Avellino, is known for its olive and olive oil production, due to its ideal terroir: rich, fertile volcanic soil and a cooler climate as a result of proximity to the Apennines mountain range. Irpinia grows the ancient variety of Ravece olives, also known as Olivona, Curatone, and Ravaiola olives. Ravece olives are prized for their low acidity, and spicy, fruity bitterness. The award-winning oil is known for the unique herbal and vegetal taste and luminous green color. As a bonus, the oil has a long shelf life.

Typically, Ravece olives are harvested by hand in October and cold pressed. They are not heated, a practice often utilized to increase yield. Low humidity and temperature is essential to the success of the oil, and therefore the olives are stored in sturdy boxes with plenty of circulation.

GATTÒ DI PATATE

Gattò is a Neapolitan corruption of the French *gâteau*, meaning cake. In the eighteenth and nineteenth centuries they were very fashionable, and came in many variations. The recipe with potatoes beat them all.

Preparation time: 30 minutes
Cooking time: 1 hour 30 minutes
Serves 6

Preheat the oven to 350°F (180°C/Gas Mark 4). Grease a 12½ x 10 inch (32 x 26 cm) cake pan and sprinkle it with about 3 tablespoons (20 g) breadcrumbs.

In a large pot of boiling water, cook the potatoes for 45 minutes, until very tender. Drain, peel, and mash into purée in a bowl.

Add 2 tablespoons (30 g) of the butter, the Parmesan, provola, salami, and parsley. Beat in 1 egg yolk at a time. Season with salt. If the mixture is too stiff, add 1 tablespoon of milk at a time until looser but still thick. Whip the egg whites into stiff peaks and gently fold into the potato mixture.

Pour half the potato mixture into the prepared cake pan. Cover with the mozzarella, and top with the remaining potato mixture. Rap the pan on the work surface a few times so that the batter settles. Smooth the surface with a spatula and lightly sprinkle with the remaining breadcrumbs. Dot the top with the remaining 5 tablespoons butter. Bake until golden brown, 30–40 minutes. Remove from the oven and let stand for 10 minutes before serving.

Potato cake

— ⅓ cup (60 g) breadcrumbs
— lb 5 oz (1.5 kg) baking potatoes
— 7 tablespoons (3½ oz /100 g) butter, at room temperature
— 1 cup (100 g) grated Parmesan cheese
— 3 oz (80 g) smoked provola cheese, cubed
— 3½ oz (100 g) salami, chopped
— 1 tablespoon chopped parsley
— 4 egg yolks
— salt
— milk
— 2 egg whites
— 5 oz (150 g) mozzarella cheese, thinly sliced

UOVA ALLA MONACHINA

Stuffed eggs

Preparation time: 40 minutes
Cooking time: 1 hour 10 minutes
Serves 4−6

For the béchamel
— 3⅓ tablespoons
   (50 g) butter
— ⅓ cup (50 g) all-purpose
   (plain) flour
— 1 cup (250 ml) milk
— ½ cup (100 ml) heavy
   (double) cream
— salt

For the eggs
— 12 eggs
— ½ cup (90 g) grated
   Parmesan cheese
— salt and pepper
— 1 cup (130 g) all-purpose
   (plain) flour
— 1 cup (115 g) breadcrumbs
— 1¼ cups (300 ml) canola oil,
   for frying

To make the béchamel: Melt the butter in a pan, add the flour, stir, and cook for 2−3 minutes (the mixture must stay pale). Stir in the milk and cream and cook, stirring, for at least 15−20 minutes. Remove from the heat, season with salt, and set aside in a warm place.

To prepare the eggs: Put 10 eggs in a saucepan and cover with cold water. Bring to a boil over high heat, then reduce the heat and cook the eggs at a gentle boil for 10 minutes. Drain and rinse under cold water to stop the cooking. Let the eggs stand in cold water for 15 minutes. Remove the shells, cut the eggs in half, and carefully remove the yolks, setting aside the egg whites.

Mash the yolks in a bowl and mix with the béchamel, Parmesan, and salt and pepper to taste. Fill half the egg whites with the yolk mixture and close with the remaining egg whites to form whole eggs.

Beat the remaining 2 eggs in a bowl. Put the flour and breadcrumbs in 2 separate bowls. Dredge the eggs first in the flour, then in the beaten eggs, and finally in the breadcrumbs.

Heat the oil in a frying pan. Fry the eggs until golden brown. Remove the eggs and drain them thoroughly on a plate lined with paper towels. Transfer to a serving dish and serve hot.

EGGPLANT

Campania is known for the long, thin eggplants (aubergines), *melanzana*, best consumed in late spring and throughout the fall. This berry is firm with a glossy skin, and is best sliced right before cooking. Salting and weighting down the slices will release any excess moisture, so as not to muddle the flavors of the dish. Once warmed through, the spongy flesh softens and turns creamy, and meltingly smooth. Eggplants can be fried, soaking up almost all oil in the pan, or roasted and baked.

The most famous eggplant dish is the *melanzane alla parmigiana* (page 171), or eggplant Parmesan. Campania, Emilia-Romagna, and Sicily all claim paternity of this dish and each area claims that the name means something different. Eggplants are sliced, salted, and weighted, and then layered with fresh mozzarella, sometimes hard-boiled eggs, and topped with a homemade tomato sauce. Occasionally the slices are tossed with breadcrumbs and fried before being layered. Flavored with fresh basil, sprinkled with grated Parmesan cheese, and baked, this dish is also served cold.

Sorrento-style cannelloni, *cannelloni alla sorrentina* (page 172) features baked and browned eggplant. Fresh egg pasta squares are rolled around a filling of eggplant, roasted red peppers, fior di latte (cow's milk mozzarella), and basil. The cannelloni are smothered with tomato sauce and baked.

A surprising dish exists on the Amalfi Coast: eggplants covered with dark chocolate. Legend states that monks in Tramonti dipped fried eggplants in dark liquor made with sugar, herbs, and spices. Over time, that was replaced by chocolate. This delicacy, *mulegnane ciucculata*, is so unusual that it is only presented during the Feast of the Assumption, in mid-August, honoring the virgin's rise to heaven. It is also showcased in the summer at the Maiori Chocolate Eggplant Festival.

The earliest written recipe for eggplant (aubergine) Parmesan was published in a cookbook from 1837.

PIZZA DI ORTAGGI

Preparation time: 40 minutes + 45 minutes rising
Cooking time: 1 hour 15 minutes
Serves 10–12

To make the dough: Dissolve the yeast in a little of the warm water in a bowl and let sit for 10–15 minutes.

Pile the flour on a work surface and make a well in the center. Pour in the yeast mixture and salt. Add the remaining water, kneading the dough until it becomes smooth and elastic, 2–3 minutes, adding more water if necessary. Cover and let the dough rise for 30 minutes.

Meanwhile, to make the filling: Heat 3 tablespoons of the oil in a large pan and sauté the onion and garlic until tender, about 5 minutes. Season with salt and pepper to taste. Add the bell peppers and sauté for 5 minutes. Add the eggplant and zucchini and cook for 5 minutes. Pour in the stock, cover the pan, and cook over low heat until the eggplant is tender, about 5 minutes. Remove the vegetable mixture from the heat and let cool, 5–7 minutes. Toss with the lemon juice and taste for seasoning.

Preheat the oven to 375°F (190°C/Gas Mark 5). Lightly oil a 10 ½-inch (26 cm) pizza pan.

Once the vegetables are cool, stir in the bread, egg, and cheese.

Divide the dough in half and roll out one portion to fit the prepared pan. Roll out the other half and set aside. Distribute the vegetable mixture evenly over the surface, leaving a 1-inch (2.5 cm) border all around. Cover with the second piece of dough, tuck under the edges, and seal. Brush the top of the pizza with the remaining 1 tablespoon oil and bake until golden brown, 50–55 minutes. Serve hot or at room temperature.

Vegetable pizza

For the dough
— 1 envelope (¼ oz/7 g) active dry yeast
— ¾ cup (200 ml) warm water
— 4¾ cups (500 g) 00 flour
— 1 teaspoon salt

For the filling
— 4 tablespoons olive oil
— 1 small yellow onion, thinly sliced
— 1 clove garlic, minced
— salt and pepper
— ½ red bell pepper, thinly sliced
— ½ green bell pepper, thinly sliced
— ½ yellow bell pepper, thinly sliced
— 3 Italian eggplants (aubergine), cut into 1-inch (2.5 cm) cubes
— 2 zucchini (courgettes), cut into ½-inch (1 cm) cubes
— ¼ cup (60 ml) chicken or vegetable stock
— 1 teaspoon lemon juice
— 2 oz (60 g) stale crustless bread, torn into pieces
— 1 egg
— 4 tablespoons grated pecorino or Parmesan cheese

RAISINS AND CURRANTS

Raisins and currants are small, sweet fruits that are dried. There are several varieties of raisins, including sultanas (which derive from vine-ripened green grapes). Currants are also a dried grape (not to be confused with the berry of the same name that grows on a bush). Zante currants (also referred to as Corinthian raisins) come from the black Corinth, a type of small, black, seedless grape. (The mispronunciation of the word Corinth resulted in the word "currant.") Whereas raisins are almost cloying sweet, currants are smaller and have a tart, punchy flavor. Both can be eaten as a snack, baked into desserts, or soaked in alcohol.

Golden raisins (sultanas) are gold-colored dried grapes that are made from varieties of seedless white-fleshed grapes. The skin of these fruits retain its sunny-colored hue thanks to a treatment of sulfur dioxide after drying, compared to the leathery skin of raisins, which darken as the raisin dries. Smaller in size, sultanas are even sweeter than raisins.

Using raisins or currants in savory dishes may derive from the Roman preference of contrasting sweet and sour cuisine. *Braciole* is a regional dish of a rolled piece of beef, stuffed with breadcrumbs, raisins, and pine nuts. When sliced, the meat resembles pinwheels. Raisins, in addition to pine nuts, are sometimes used in Neapolitan meatballs. The dried fruit does a fine job of adding a punchy flavor to pizza filling, alongside the quieter escarole, in *pizza di scarola* (page 261). *Baccalà alla napoletana* is a dish of sautéed salt cod with tomato, black olives, raisins, pine nuts, capers, and garlic.

Grape vines grow throughout the region of Avellino.

PIZZA DI SCAROLA

Preparation time: 30 minutes + 30 minutes rising
Cooking time: 50 minutes
Serves 6−8

To make the dough: Dissolve the yeast, sugar, and a little warm water in a bowl. Let stand for 10 minutes.

Pile the flour on a work surface and make a well in the center. Add the butter, salt, and pepper to taste and knead together, adding warm water as needed to obtain a smooth dough. Place in a bowl brushed with oil, cover, and let rise for 20−25 minutes.

To make the filling: Bring a large pot of water to a boil. Add the escarole in batches and cook until just tender, 2−3 minutes. Plunge into a large bowl of cold water. Drain and squeeze dry. Set aside.

Heat the oil in a frying pan. Brown the garlic, then discard it. Stir in the anchovies, capers, olives, currants, pine nuts, chili flakes, and the blanched escarole and cook for 5 minutes. Season with black pepper. Remove from the heat and let cool.

Preheat the oven to 375°F (190°C/Gas Mark 5).

Divide the dough in half, with one piece slightly larger than the other. Roll out the larger half to line the bottom and sides of a 10-inch (25 cm) cake pan. Use tongs to transfer the escarole mixture to the crust, leaving any liquid in the frying pan. Roll out the second piece of dough to the diameter of the pan, place over the filling, tuck in the edges, and press together to seal.

Brush the crust with the beaten egg, sprinkle with salt, cut a few vents, and bake for 50 minutes. Remove from the oven and serve warm or cold.

Escarole pizza

For the dough
— 1 envelope (¼ oz/7 g)
    active dry yeast
— pinch of granulated sugar
— warm water, as needed
— 3¾ cups (400 g) 00 flour
— 14 tablespoons (7 oz/200 g)
    butter, at room temperature
— pinch of salt
— pepper
— olive oil, for coating the bowl

For the filling
— 3 medium heads (about
    1 lb/500 g each) escarole,
    trimmed and cut into 1-inch
    (2.5 cm) ribbons
— 3 tablespoons olive oil
— 1 clove garlic, peeled
    but whole
— 3 oz (80 g) anchovy fillets,
    chopped
— ¼ cup (50 g) capers
— 10 oz (300 g) pitted
    Gaeta olives
— 4 tablespoons dried currants
— 4 tablespoons pine nuts
— ¼ teaspoon crushed chili
    pepper flakes
— black pepper

— 1 egg, beaten
— salt

HAZELNUTS

Sometimes known as filberts, *nocciole*, or hazelnuts, are an intensely flavored, pale yellow nut covered by flaky brown skin. Best served roasted with the skins rubbed off, hazelnuts are ubiquitous in Campania, a region with established hazelnut groves.

Beginning in the third century BC, various writers and poets, including Virgil, wrote about the illustrious hazelnut. The nut was so celebrated that it can be seen on a fresco in Herculaneum, an ancient Roman town destroyed by Mt. Vesuvius in 79 AD.

Until more recently, hazelnuts were exported from Campania, specifically the port of Naples, to France and Holland. The hazelnut trade was so essential to Campania that until the end of the seventeenth century there were specialized offices that measured the nuts, providing quality control. Campania was previously responsible for about 50 percent of Italian production. Because of Campania's excellent and fertile volcanic soil and climate, hazelnuts continue to flourish in this region.

Besides Avellino, Salerno boasts an excellent variety, *nocciola di Giffoni*, which dates back to Roman times: The Naples National Archaelogical Museum includes charred remains of this variety. This variety has now achieved PGI (protected geographical indication) status.

A large percentage of hazelnut production goes to making confections and liqueurs.

Pages 266—267:
The sun breaks through the clouds to illuminate the landscape of Benevento.

PASTA BASE PER LA PIZZA

Preparation time: 15 minutes + 35 minutes rising
Cooking time: 20 minutes
Makes enough for 1 large pizza or 2 small pizzas

Dissolve the yeast in a little of the warm water in a bowl. Add 5 tablespoons of the flour, mix well, adding more water, if needed, to turn the mixture into a paste. Let stand for 15–20 minutes.

Pile the remaining flour on a work surface and make a well in the center. Add the salt and yeast mixture to the well and knead the mixture vigorously, about 2 minutes, adding the remaining warm water a little at a time, as needed to obtain a soft, supple dough. Let rise in a warm place until doubled in volume, about 20 minutes.

To make two small pizzas, grease two 8–9-inch (20–24 cm) pizza pans. Divide the dough into 2 balls and roll each out on a floured surface (or pan with damp hands) and line the pizza pans.

To make one large pizza, grease a 14–15-inch (35–38 cm) pizza pan. Roll or pat the whole ball of dough and fit it into the pizza pan.

Flatten the dough by hitting the surface with the palm of the hands until the dough covers the bottom of the pan(s), cover with a kitchen towel, and let rise in a warm place for at least 20 minutes.

Pizza dough

— 1 envelope (¼ oz/7 g) active dry yeast
— 1 cup (240 ml) warm water, plus more as needed
— 2⅓ cups (250 g) 00 flour or sifted all-purpose (plain) flour
— pinch of salt
— olive oil, for brushing the pan

INDEX

Page numbers in bold refer to the illustrations

RECIPE NOTES

Butter should always be unsalted.

Unless otherwise stated, all herbs are fresh and parsley is flat-leaf parsley.

Pepper is always freshly ground black pepper, unless otherwise specified.

Vegetables and fruits are assumed to be medium size, unless otherwise specified.

Eggs are assumed to be large, unless otherwise specified. (For the UK, eggs are medium.)

Milk is always whole, unless otherwise specified.

Garlic cloves are assumed to be large; use two if yours are small.

Prosciutto refers exclusively to raw, dry-cured ham.

Cooking and preparation times are for guidance only, as individual stoves and ovens vary. If using a convection (fan) oven, follow the manufacturer's instructions concerning oven temperatures.

To test whether your deep-frying oil is hot enough, use a deep-frying thermometer. Alternatively, add a cube of stale bread. If it browns in 30 seconds, the temperature is 350°–375°F (180°–190°C), about right for most frying. Exercise caution when deep-frying: Add the food carefully to avoid splashing, wear long sleeves, and never leave the pan unattended.

Some recipes include raw or very lightly cooked eggs. These should be avoided particularly by the elderly, infants, pregnant women, convalescents, and anyone with an impaired immune system.

Phaidon Press Limited
Regent's Wharf
All Saints Street
London N1 9PA

Phaidon Press Inc.
65 Bleecker Street
New York, NY 10012

phaidon.com

First published 2017
© 2017 Phaidon Press Limited

ISBN 978 0 7148 7385 5

Naples and the Amalfi Coast originates
from *Il cucchiaio d'argento La Grande
Cucina Regionale Campania*, first published
in 2007.

© Editorial Domus S.p.a

A CIP catalogue record for this book is
available from the British Library and the
Library of Congress.

Commissioning Editor: Emilia Terragni
Project Editor: Laura Loesch-Quintin
Production Controller: Leonie Kellman

Narrative text by Adelaide Mueller
Designed by Sonya Dyakova
Photographs by Simon Bajada
Illustrations by Beppe Giacobbe
Translated by Mary Consonni
Printed in China

The publisher would like to thank Clelia
d'Onofrio, Carmen Figini, Adelaide
Mueller, Kate Slate, Cecilia Molinari,
Luísa Martelo, and lariggiola.se for their
contributions to the book.